GRAPHIC BIOGRAPHIES

MATTHEW HENSON
Arctic Adventurer

by B. A. Hoena
illustrated by
Phil Miller and Charles Barnett III

Consultant:
Genevieve LeMoine
Curator/Registrar
The Peary-MacMillan Arctic Museum
Brunswick, Maine

Capstone
press

Mankato, Minnesota

Graphic Library is published by Capstone Press,
1710 Roe Crest Drive, North Mankato, Minnesota 56003.
www.capstonepub.com

Library of Congress Cataloging-in-Publication Data
Hoena, B. A.
Matthew Henson : Arctic adventurer / by B.A. Hoena ; illustrated by Phil Miller and Charles Barnett III.
p. cm.—(Graphic library. Graphic biographies)
Includes bibliographical references and index.
ISBN: 978-0-7368-4634-9 (hardcover)
ISBN: 978-0-7368-6198-4 (softcover)
1. Henson, Matthew Alexander, 1866–1955—Juvenile literature. 2. African-American explorers—Biography—Juvenile literature. 3. North Pole—Discovery and exploration—Juvenile literature. I. Miller, Phil, ill. II. Barnett, Charles, III, ill. III. Title. IV. Series.
G635.H4H642 2006
910'.92—dc22 2005005774

Summary: In graphic novel format, tells the life story of explorer Matthew Henson and his expedition to the North Pole with Robert Peary.

Art Director
Jason Knudson

Designer
Bob Lentz

Colorist
Scott Thoms

Editor
Tom Adamson

Editor's note: Direct quotations from primary sources are indicated by a yellow background.

Direct quotations appear on the following pages:
Pages 4, 5, 6, 8, 10, 11, 14, 20 (Henson's line), 22, 25, 26, from *Dark Companion* by Bradley Robinson (New York, R. M. McBride, 1948).
Page 13, from *The North Pole* by Robert E. Peary (New York: Cooper Square Press, 2001).
Pages 16, 17, from *North Pole Legacy* by S. Allen Counter (Amherst: University of Massachusetts Press, 1991).
Page 20 (Peary's line), from "Matthew Henson" by Donald D. MacMillan (*The Explorers Journal* Fall 1955).

Printed in the United States 5461

TABLE OF CONTENTS

Chapter 1

Young Adventurer

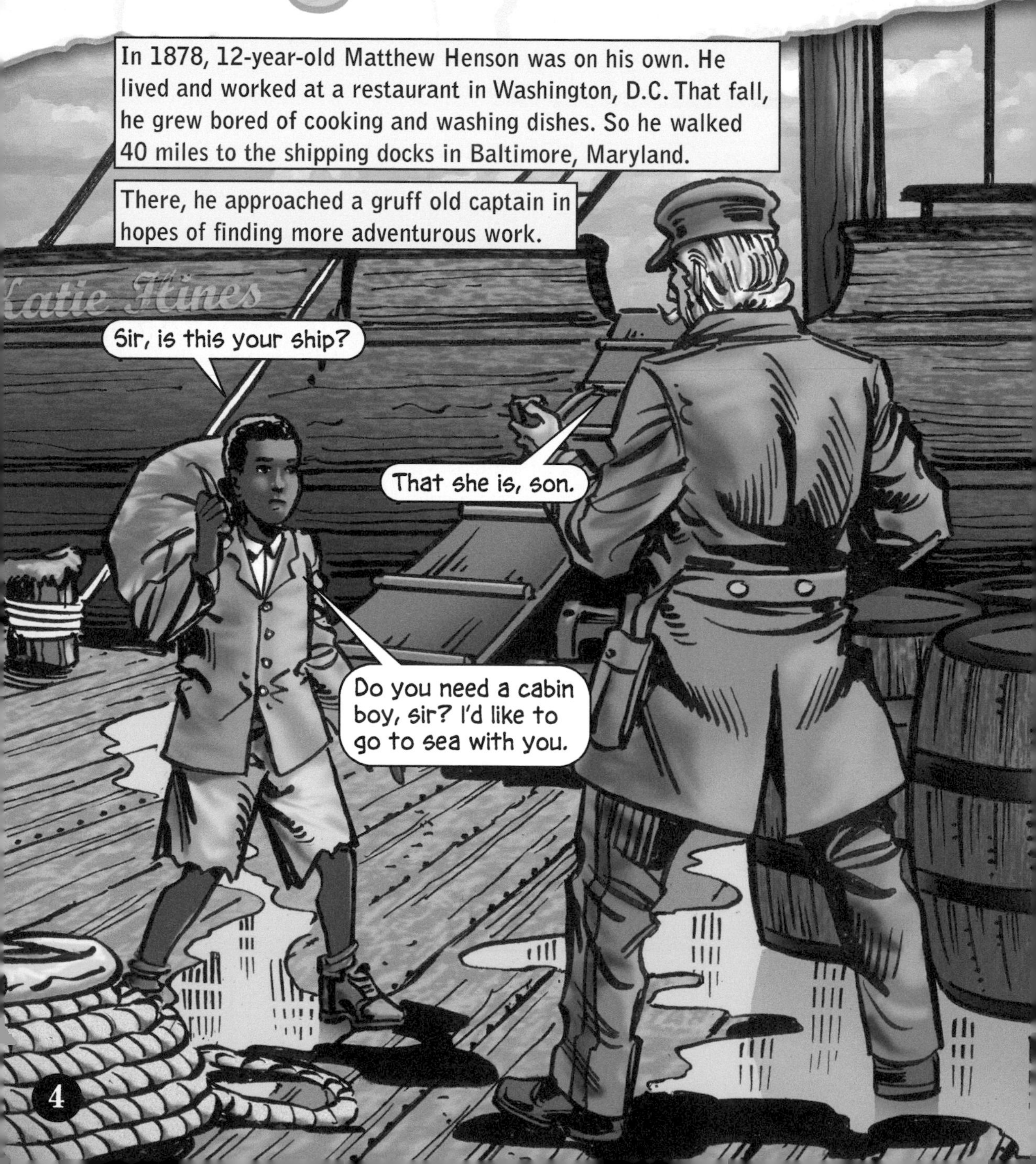
In 1878, 12-year-old Matthew Henson was on his own. He lived and worked at a restaurant in Washington, D.C. That fall, he grew bored of cooking and washing dishes. So he walked 40 miles to the shipping docks in Baltimore, Maryland.
There, he approached a gruff old captain in hopes of finding more adventurous work.
Sir, is this your ship?
That she is, son.
Do you need a cabin boy, sir? I'd like to go to sea with you.

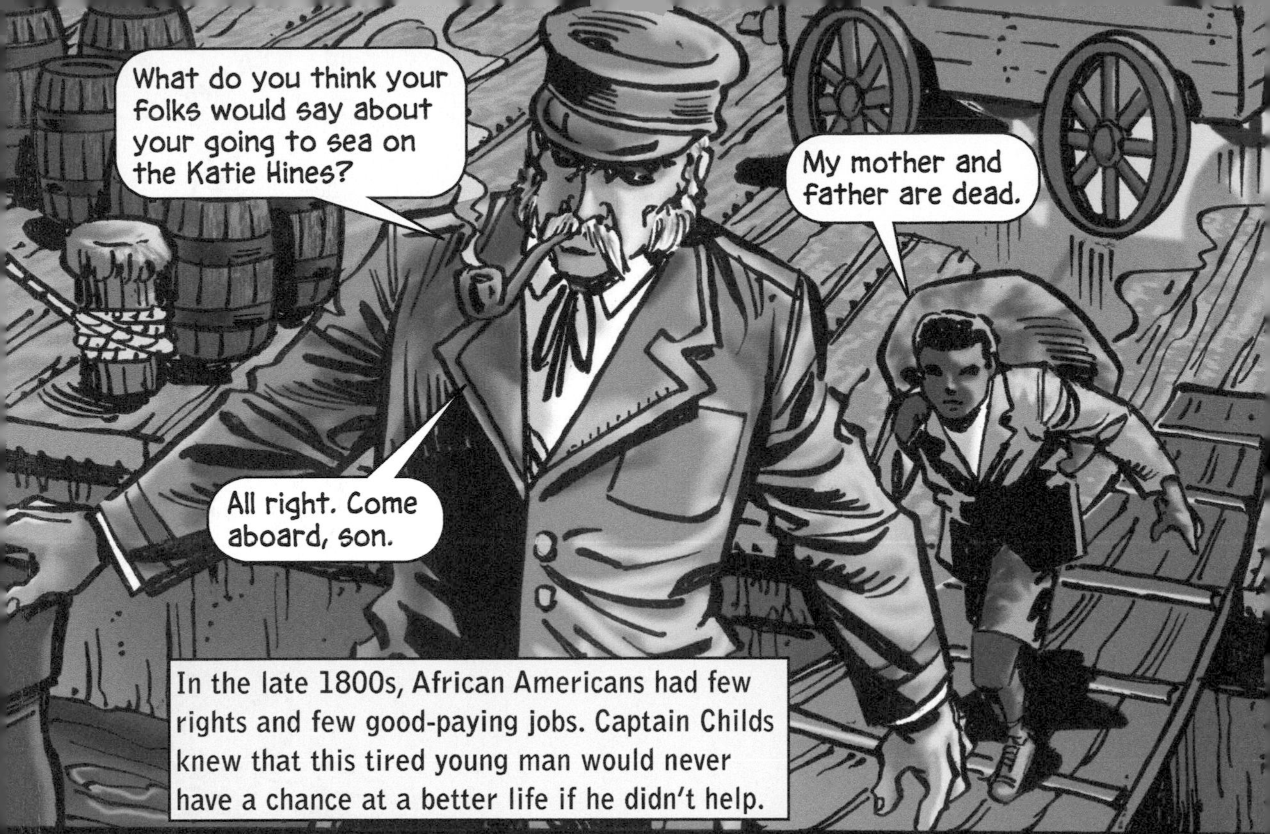
What do you think your folks would say about your going to sea on the Katie Hines?
My mother and father are dead.
All right. Come aboard, son.
In the late 1800s, African Americans had few rights and few good-paying jobs. Captain Childs knew that this tired young man would never have a chance at a better life if he didn't help.

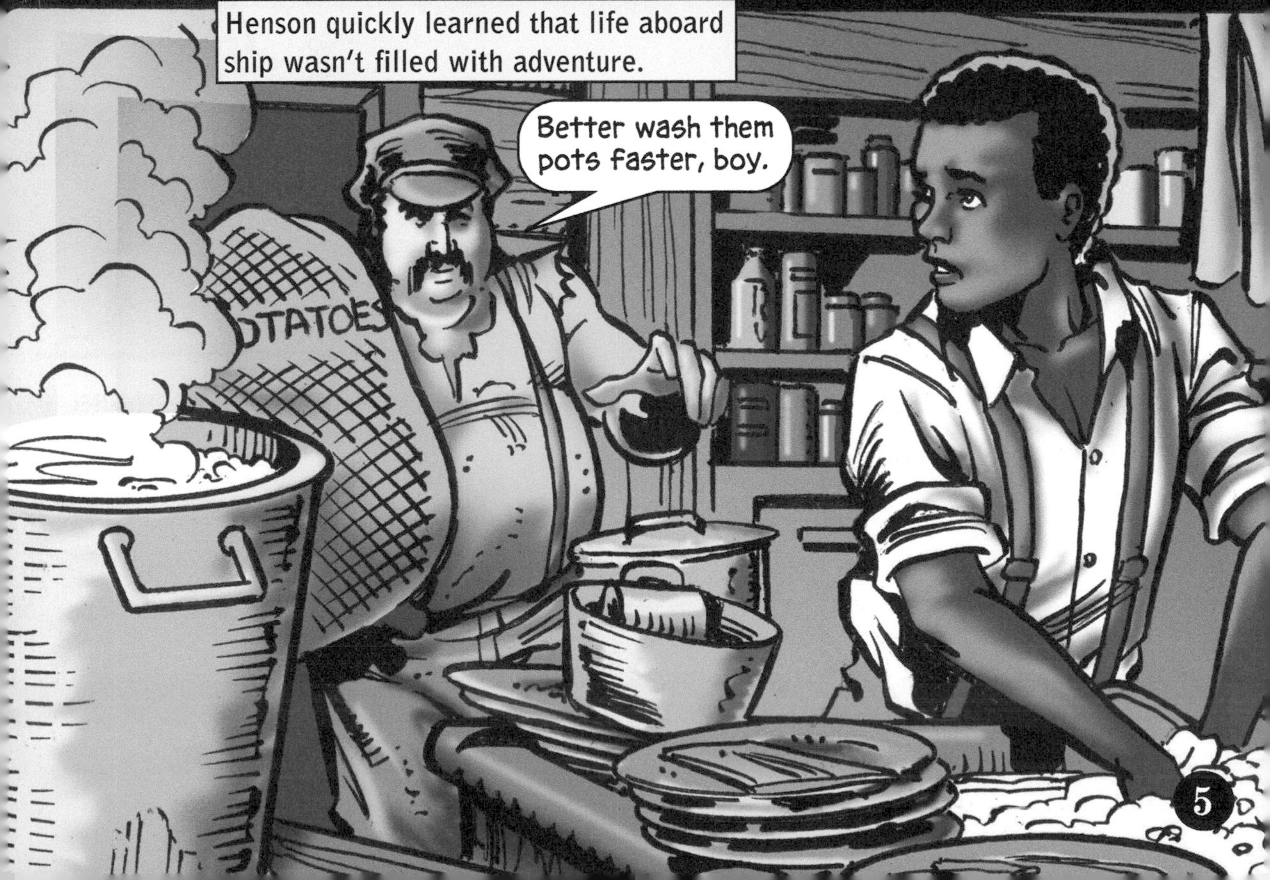
Henson quickly learned that life aboard ship wasn't filled with adventure.
Better wash them pots faster, boy.

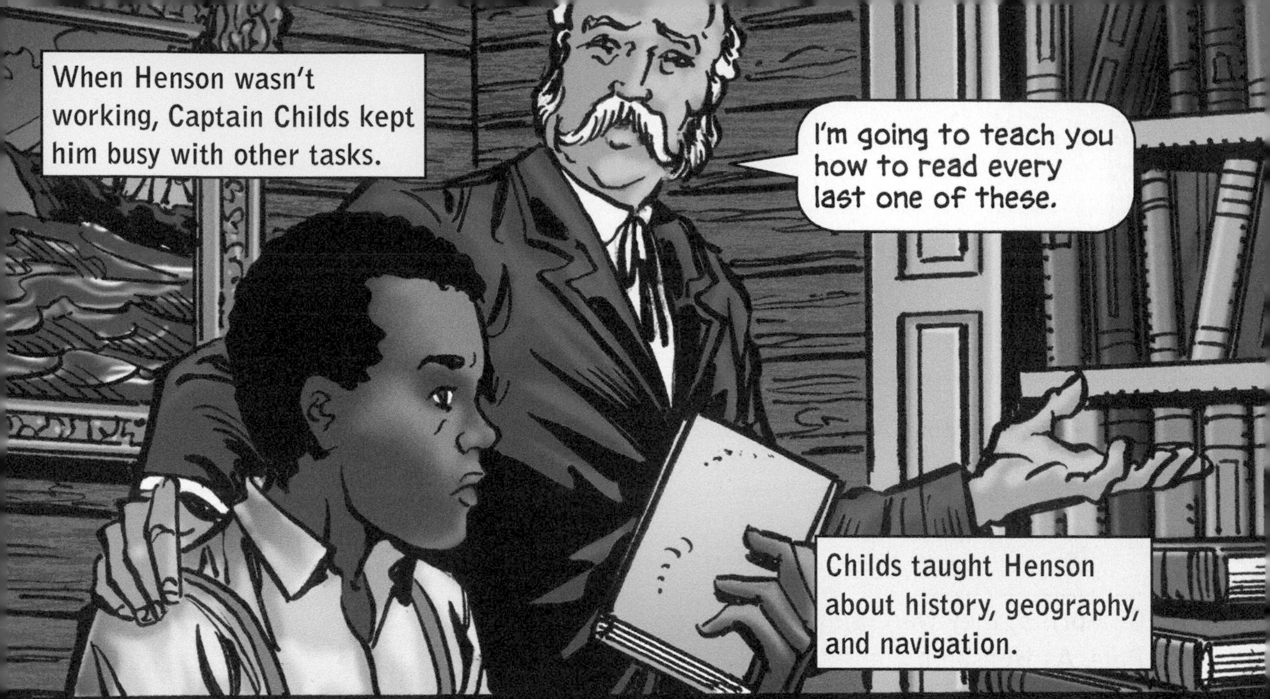
When Henson wasn't working, Captain Childs kept him busy with other tasks.
I'm going to teach you how to read every last one of these.
Childs taught Henson about history, geography, and navigation.

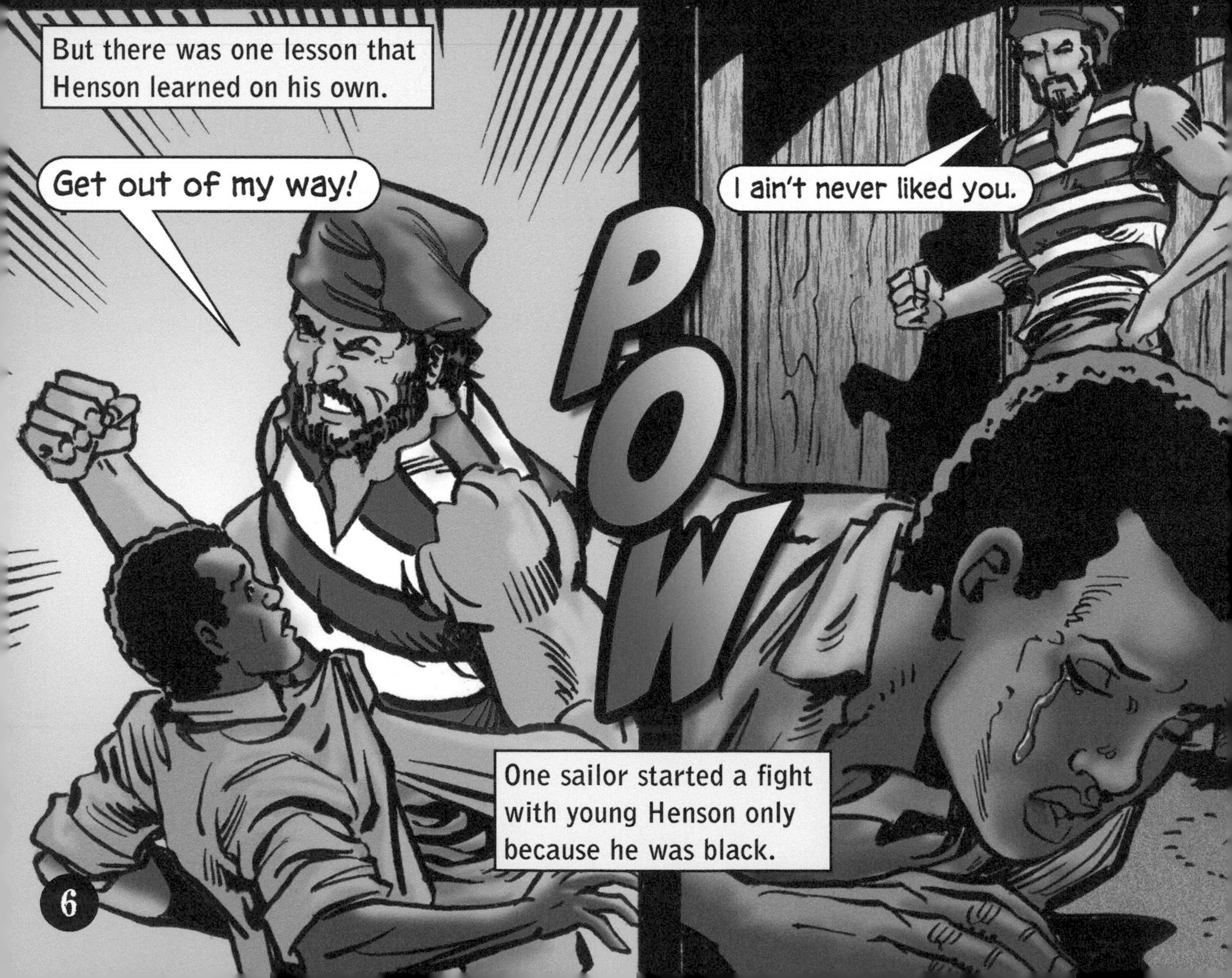
But there was one lesson that Henson learned on his own.
Get out of my way!
I ain't never liked you.
POW
One sailor started a fight with young Henson only because he was black.

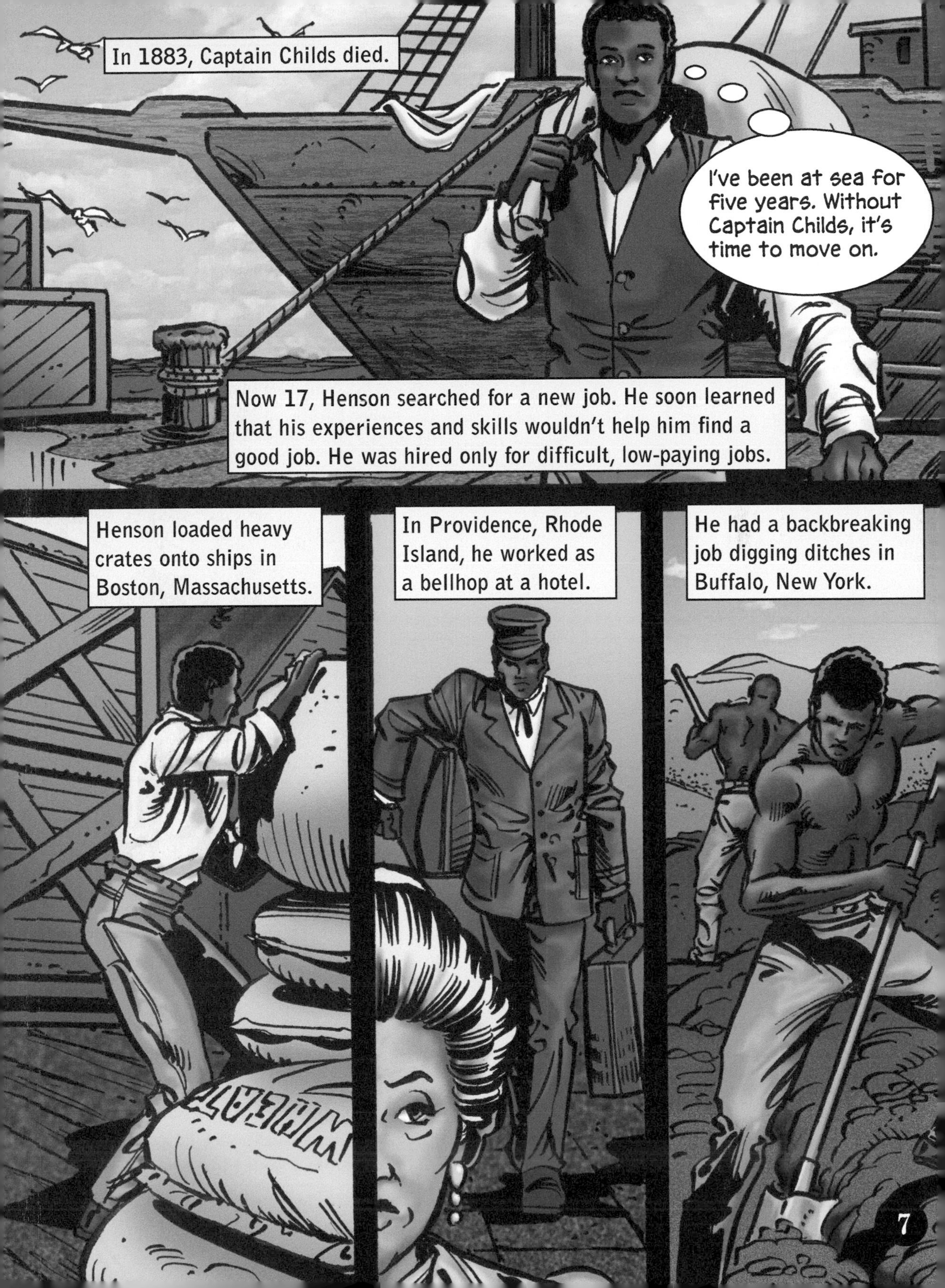
In 1883, Captain Childs died.
I've been at sea for five years. Without Captain Childs, it's time to move on.
Now 17, Henson searched for a new job. He soon learned that his experiences and skills wouldn't help him find a good job. He was hired only for difficult, low-paying jobs.
Henson loaded heavy crates onto ships in Boston, Massachusetts.
In Providence, Rhode Island, he worked as a bellhop at a hotel.
He had a backbreaking job digging ditches in Buffalo, New York.

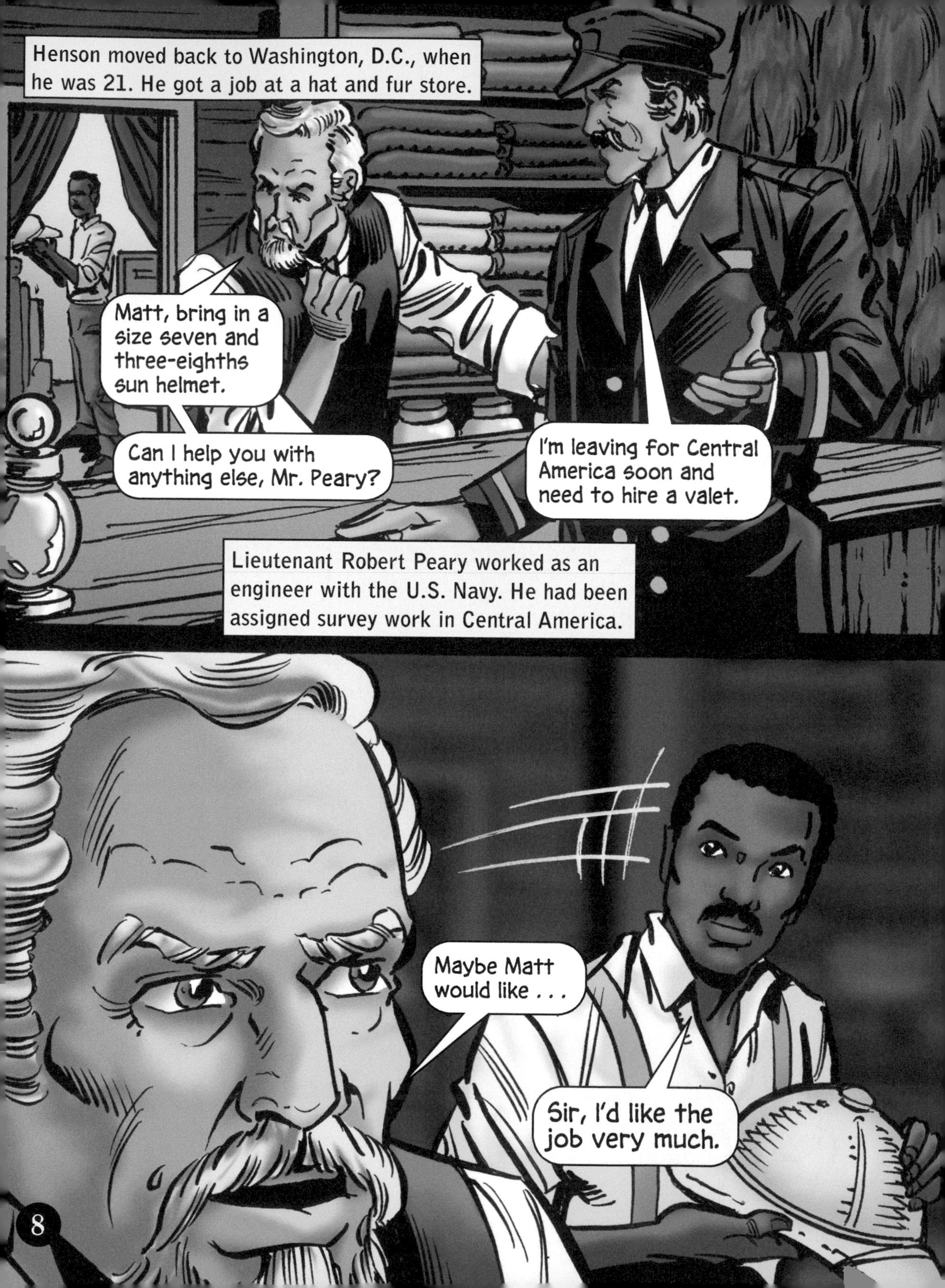
Henson moved back to Washington, D.C., when he was 21. He got a job at a hat and fur store.
Matt, bring in a size seven and three-eighths sun helmet.
Can I help you with anything else, Mr. Peary?
I'm leaving for Central America soon and need to hire a valet.
Lieutenant Robert Peary worked as an engineer with the U.S. Navy. He had been assigned survey work in Central America.
Maybe Matt would like . . .
Sir, I'd like the job very much.

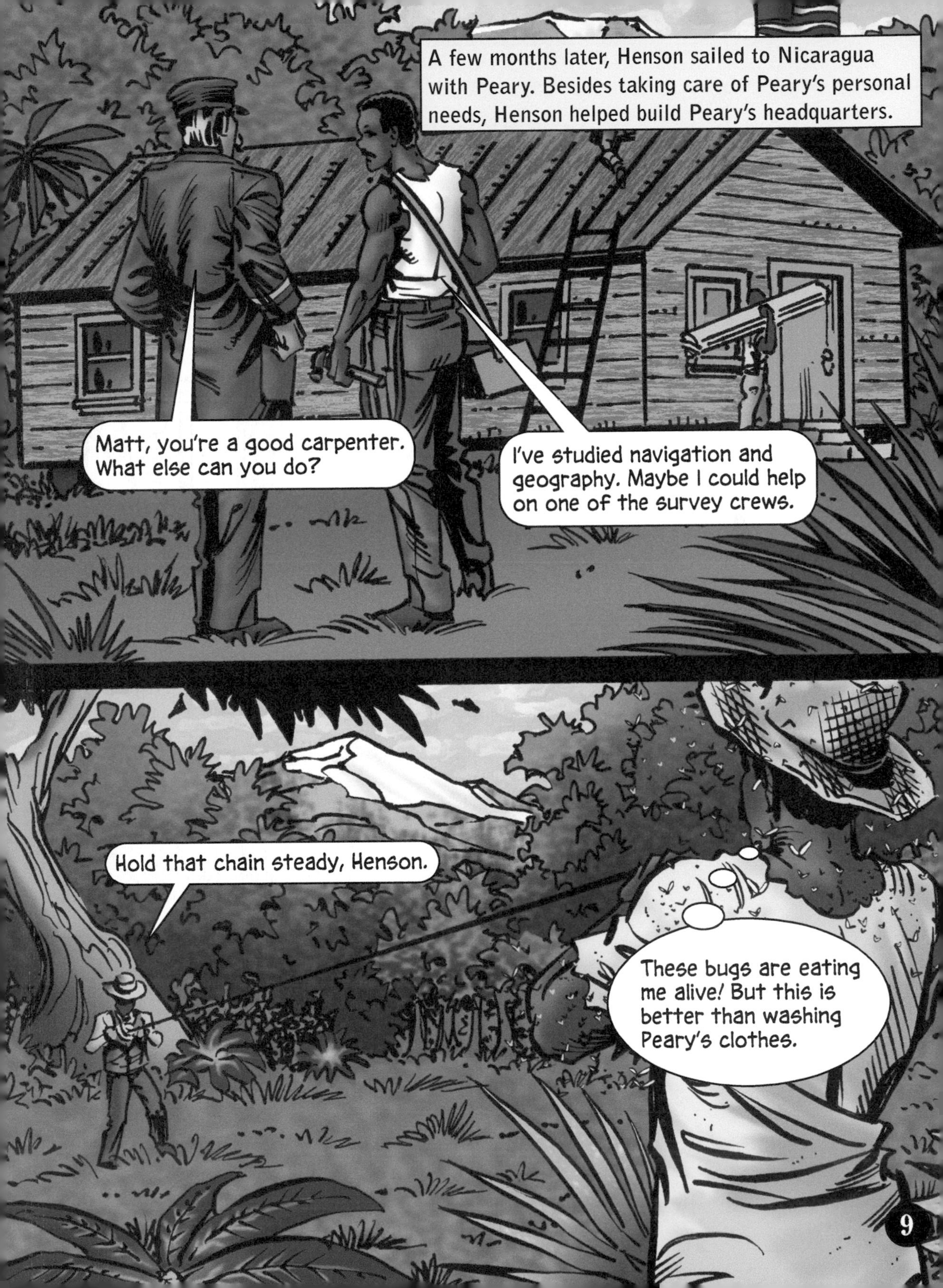
A few months later, Henson sailed to Nicaragua with Peary. Besides taking care of Peary's personal needs, Henson helped build Peary's headquarters.
Matt, you're a good carpenter. What else can you do?
I've studied navigation and geography. Maybe I could help on one of the survey crews.
Hold that chain steady, Henson.
These bugs are eating me alive! But this is better than washing Peary's clothes.

Chapter 2
Peary's Dream

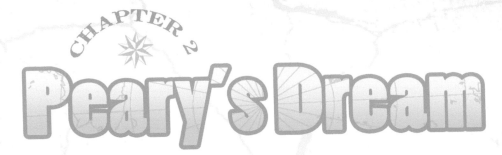

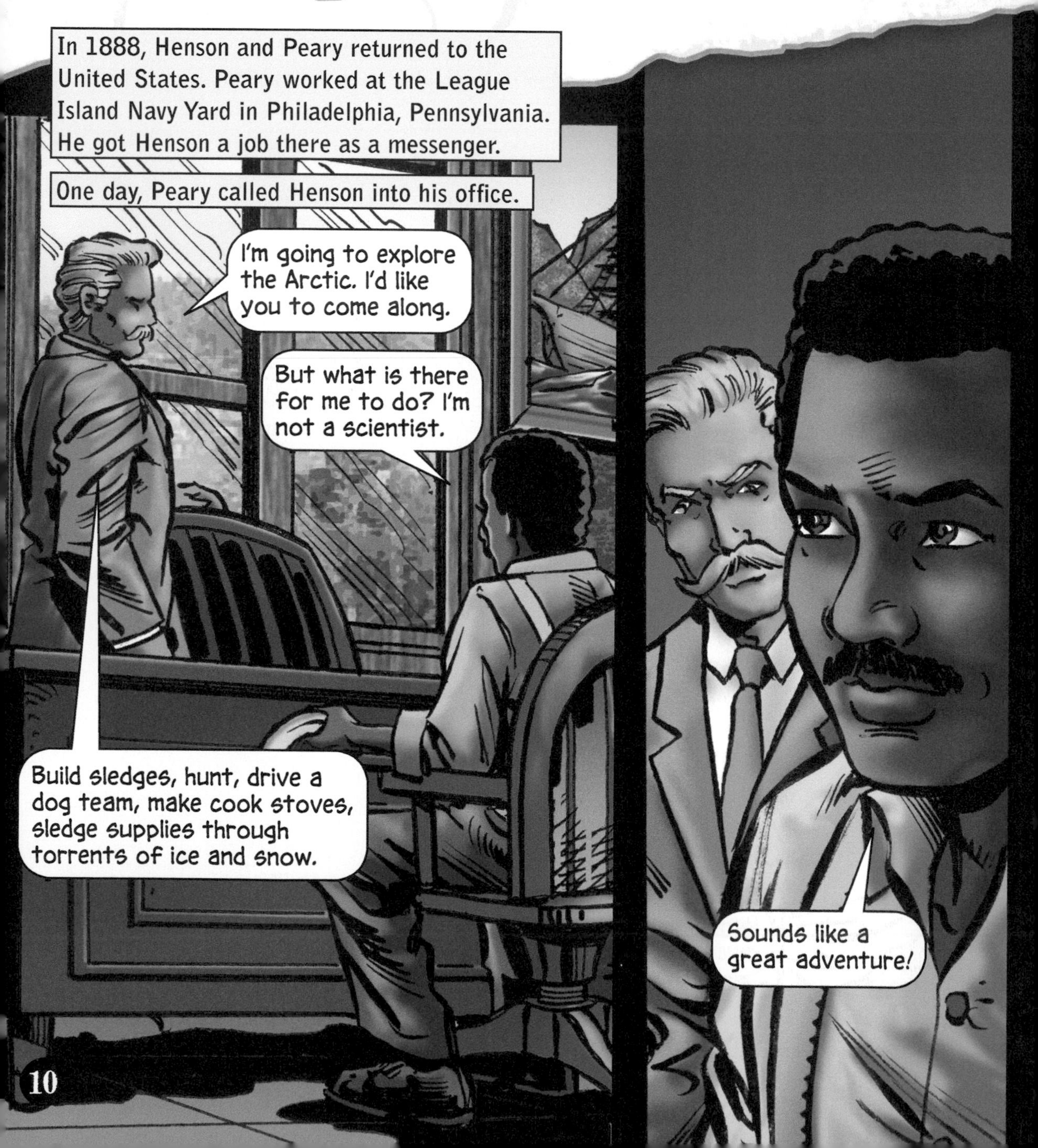
In 1888, Henson and Peary returned to the United States. Peary worked at the League Island Navy Yard in Philadelphia, Pennsylvania. He got Henson a job there as a messenger.
One day, Peary called Henson into his office.
I'm going to explore the Arctic. I'd like you to come along.
But what is there for me to do? I'm not a scientist.
Build sledges, hunt, drive a dog team, make cook stoves, sledge supplies through torrents of ice and snow.
Sounds like a great adventure!

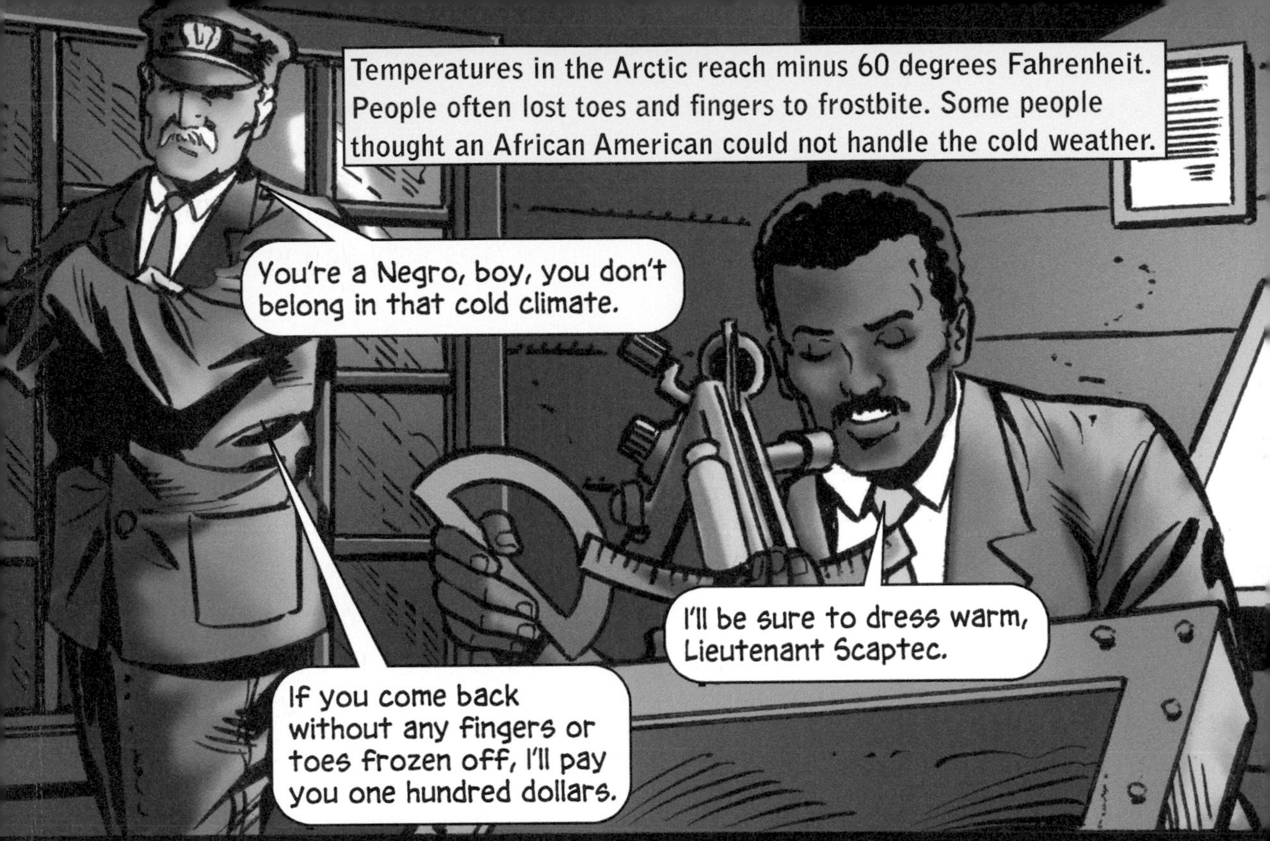
Temperatures in the Arctic reach minus 60 degrees Fahrenheit. People often lost toes and fingers to frostbite. Some people thought an African American could not handle the cold weather.
You're a Negro, boy, you don't belong in that cold climate.
If you come back without any fingers or toes frozen off, I'll pay you one hundred dollars.
I'll be sure to dress warm, Lieutenant Scaptec.

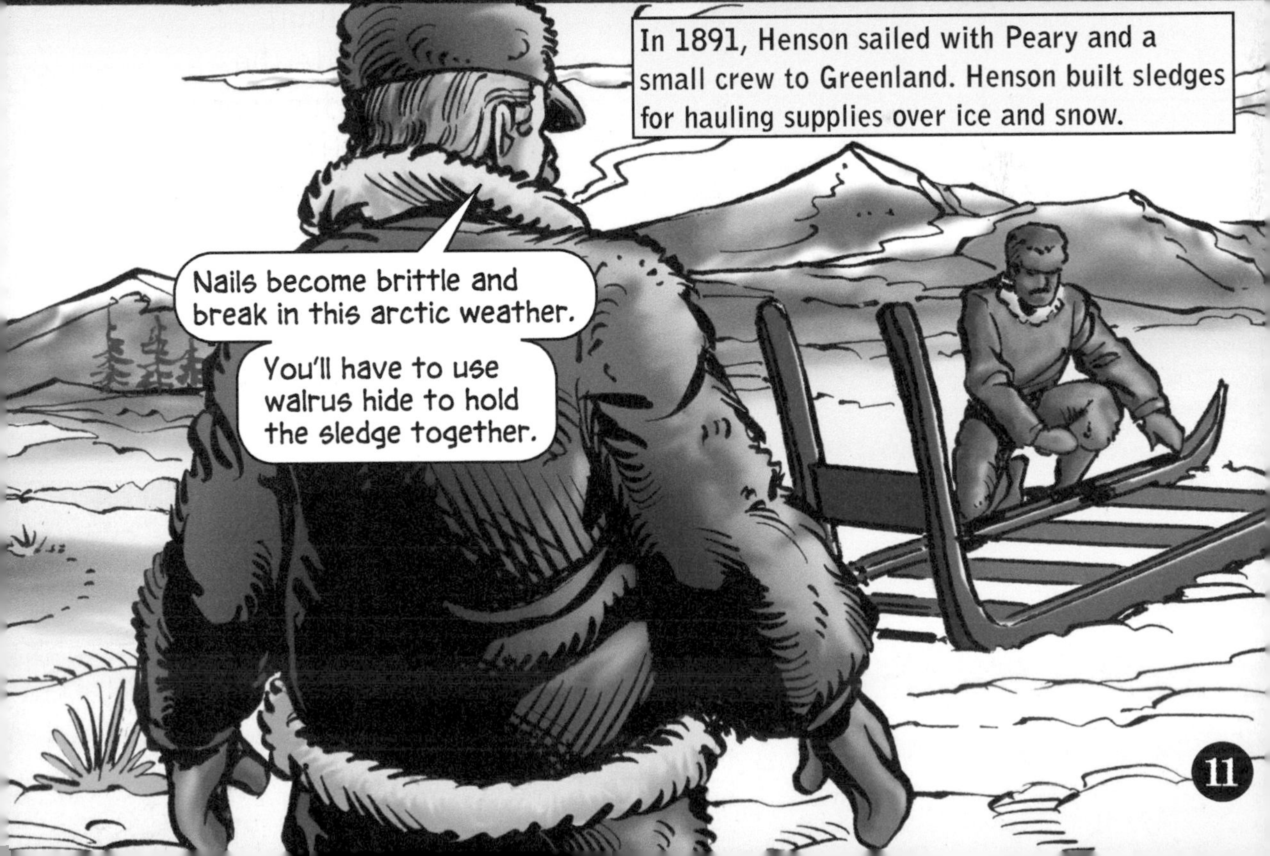
In 1891, Henson sailed with Peary and a small crew to Greenland. Henson built sledges for hauling supplies over ice and snow.
Nails become brittle and break in this arctic weather.
You'll have to use walrus hide to hold the sledge together.

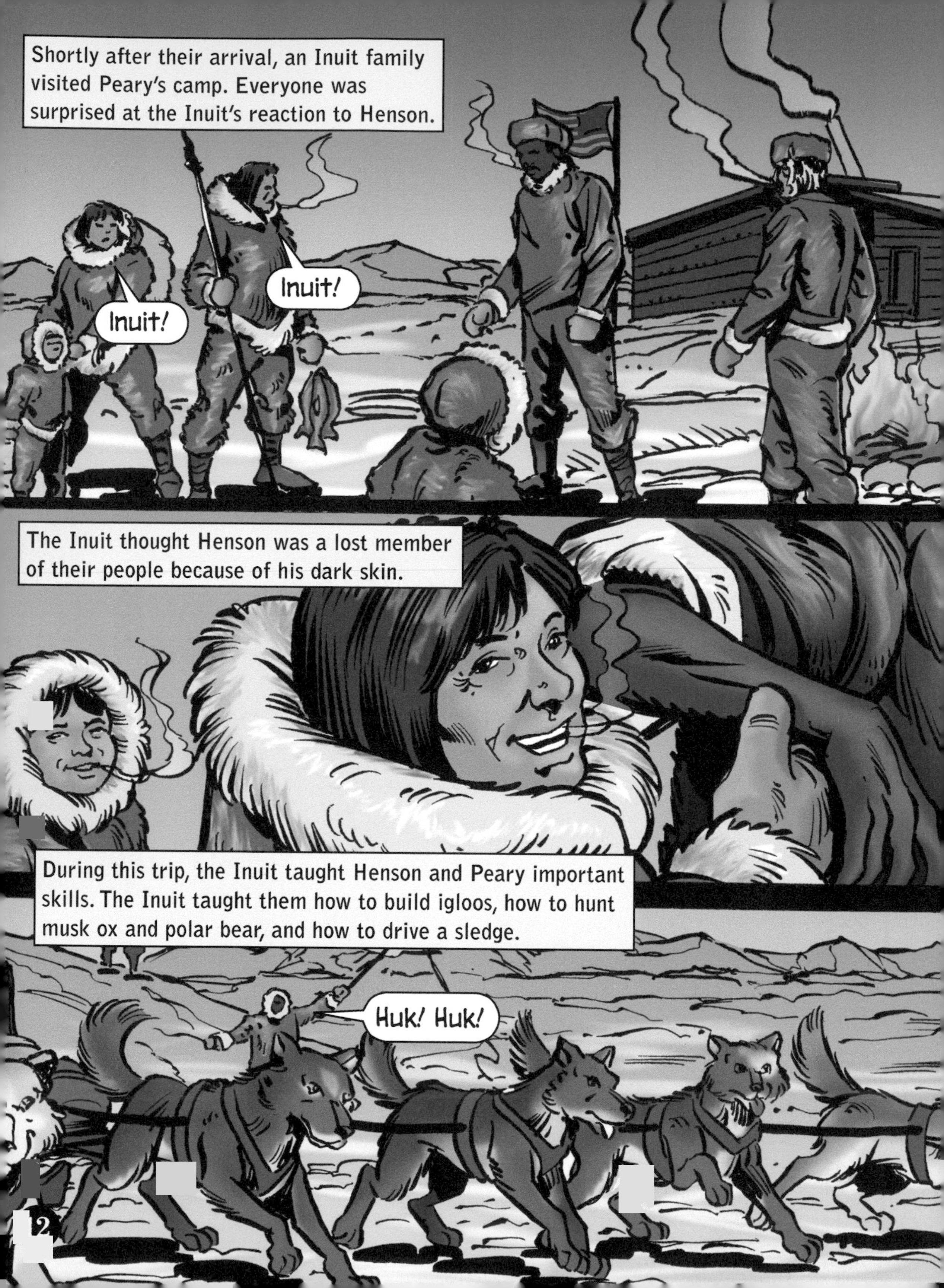
Shortly after their arrival, an Inuit family visited Peary's camp. Everyone was surprised at the Inuit's reaction to Henson.
Inuit!
Inuit!
The Inuit thought Henson was a lost member of their people because of his dark skin.
During this trip, the Inuit taught Henson and Peary important skills. The Inuit taught them how to build igloos, how to hunt musk ox and polar bear, and how to drive a sledge.
Huk! Huk!

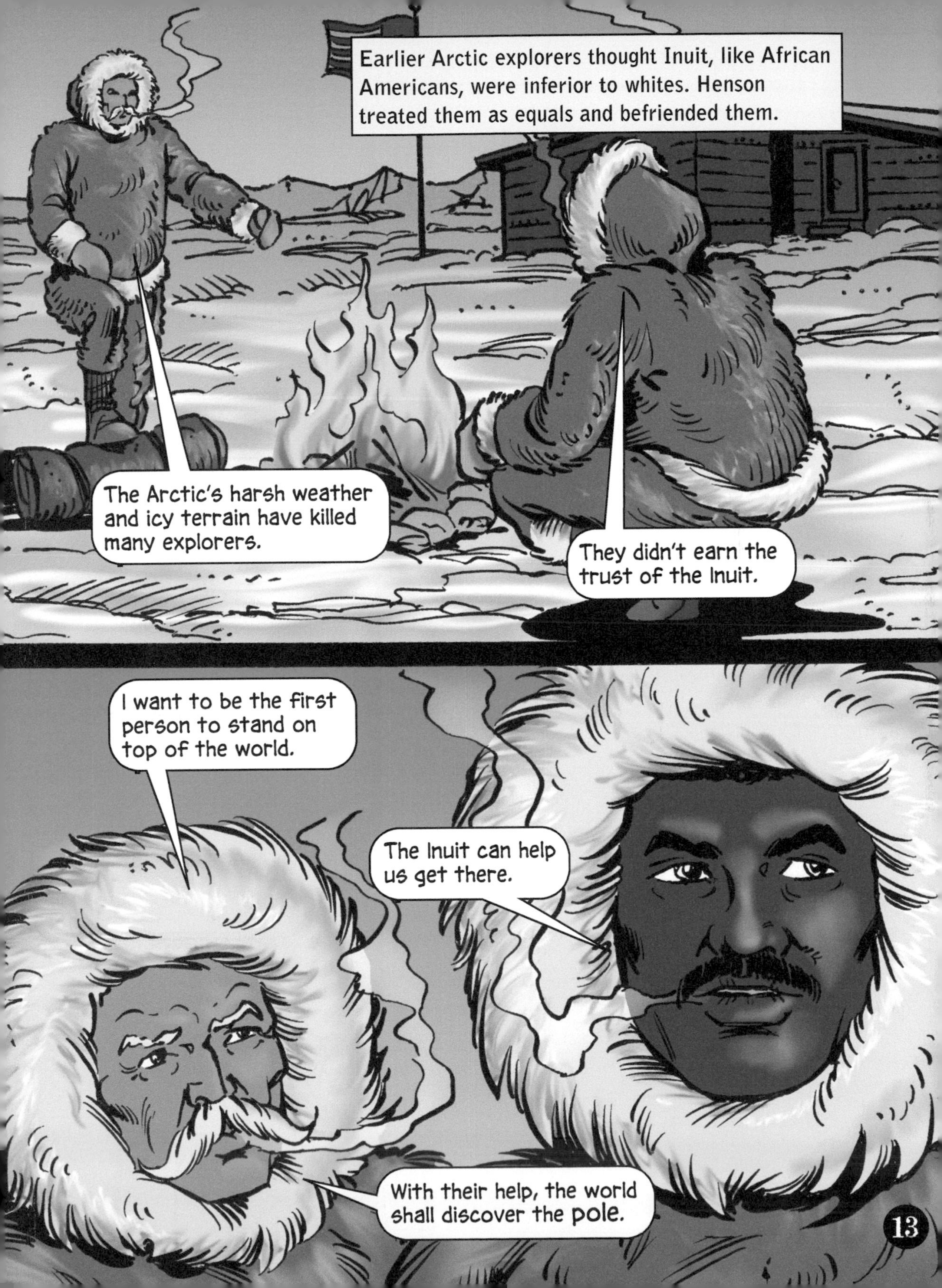
Earlier Arctic explorers thought Inuit, like African Americans, were inferior to whites. Henson treated them as equals and befriended them.
The Arctic's harsh weather and icy terrain have killed many explorers.
They didn't earn the trust of the Inuit.
I want to be the first person to stand on top of the world.
The Inuit can help us get there.
With their help, the world shall discover the pole.

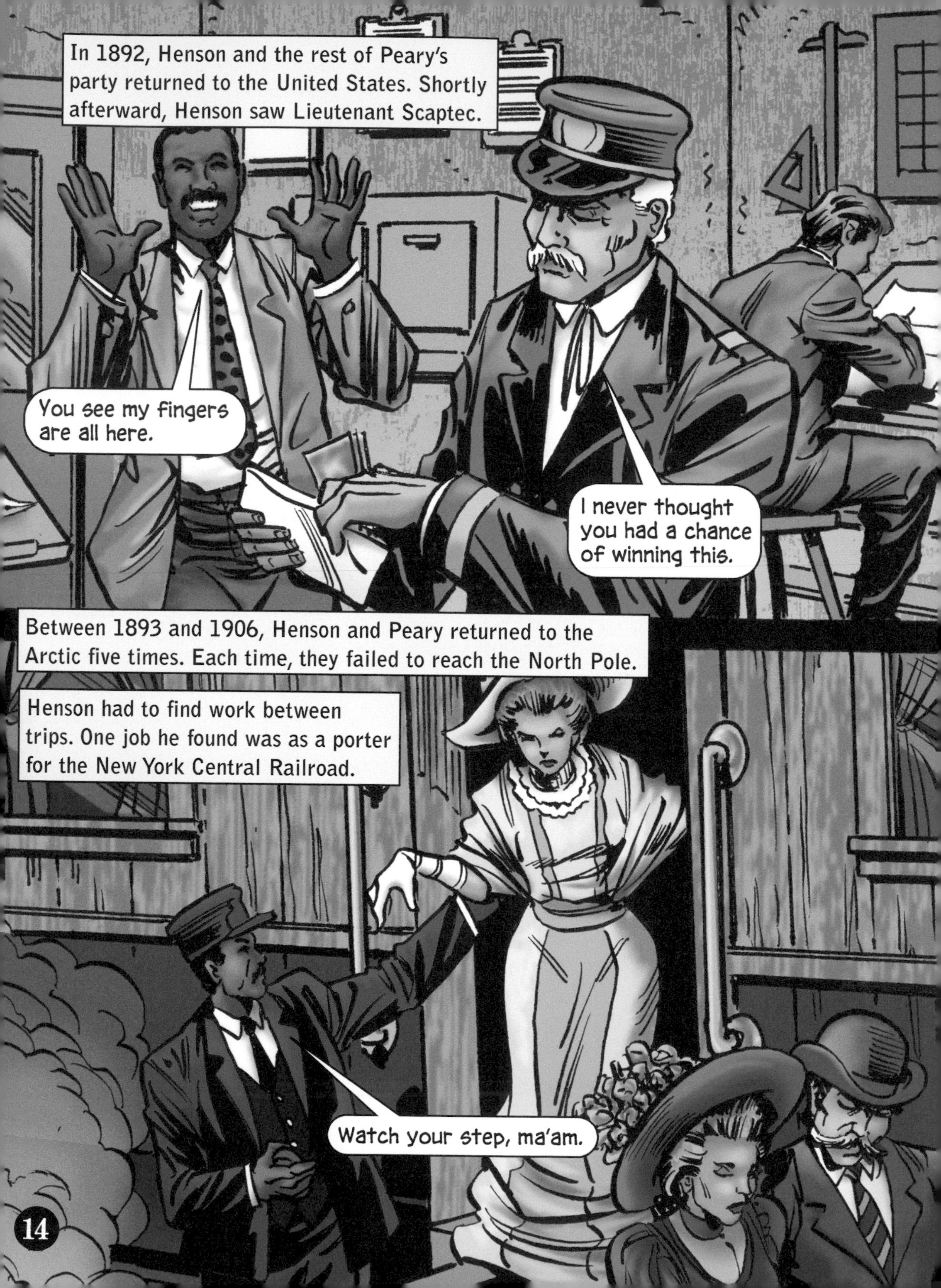
In 1892, Henson and the rest of Peary's party returned to the United States. Shortly afterward, Henson saw Lieutenant Scaptec.
You see my fingers are all here.
I never thought you had a chance of winning this.
Between 1893 and 1906, Henson and Peary returned to the Arctic five times. Each time, they failed to reach the North Pole.
Henson had to find work between trips. One job he found was as a porter for the New York Central Railroad.
Watch your step, ma'am.

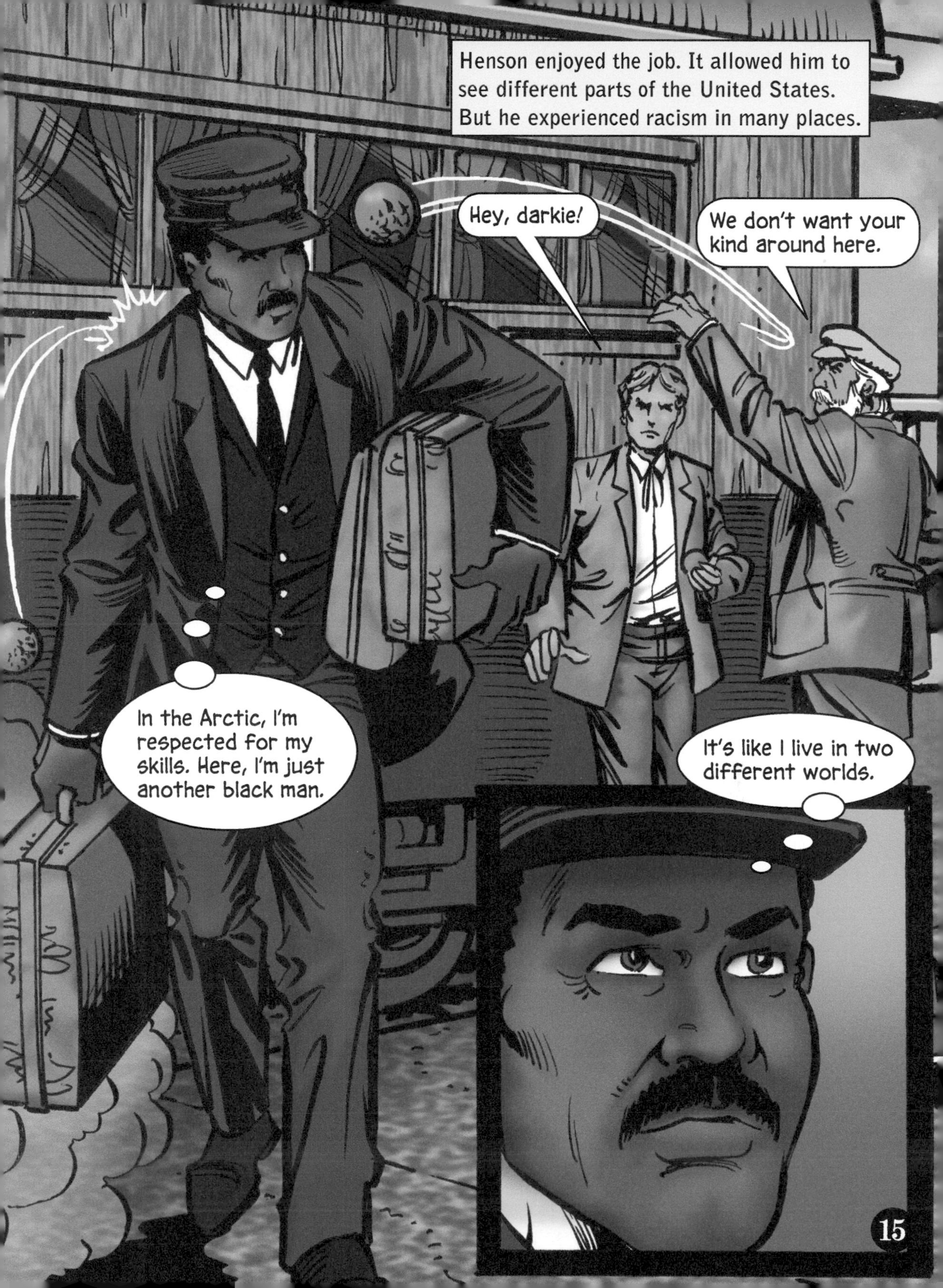
Henson enjoyed the job. It allowed him to see different parts of the United States. But he experienced racism in many places.
Hey, darkie!
We don't want your kind around here.
In the Arctic, I'm respected for my skills. Here, I'm just another black man.
It's like I live in two different worlds.

Chapter 3

The North Pole

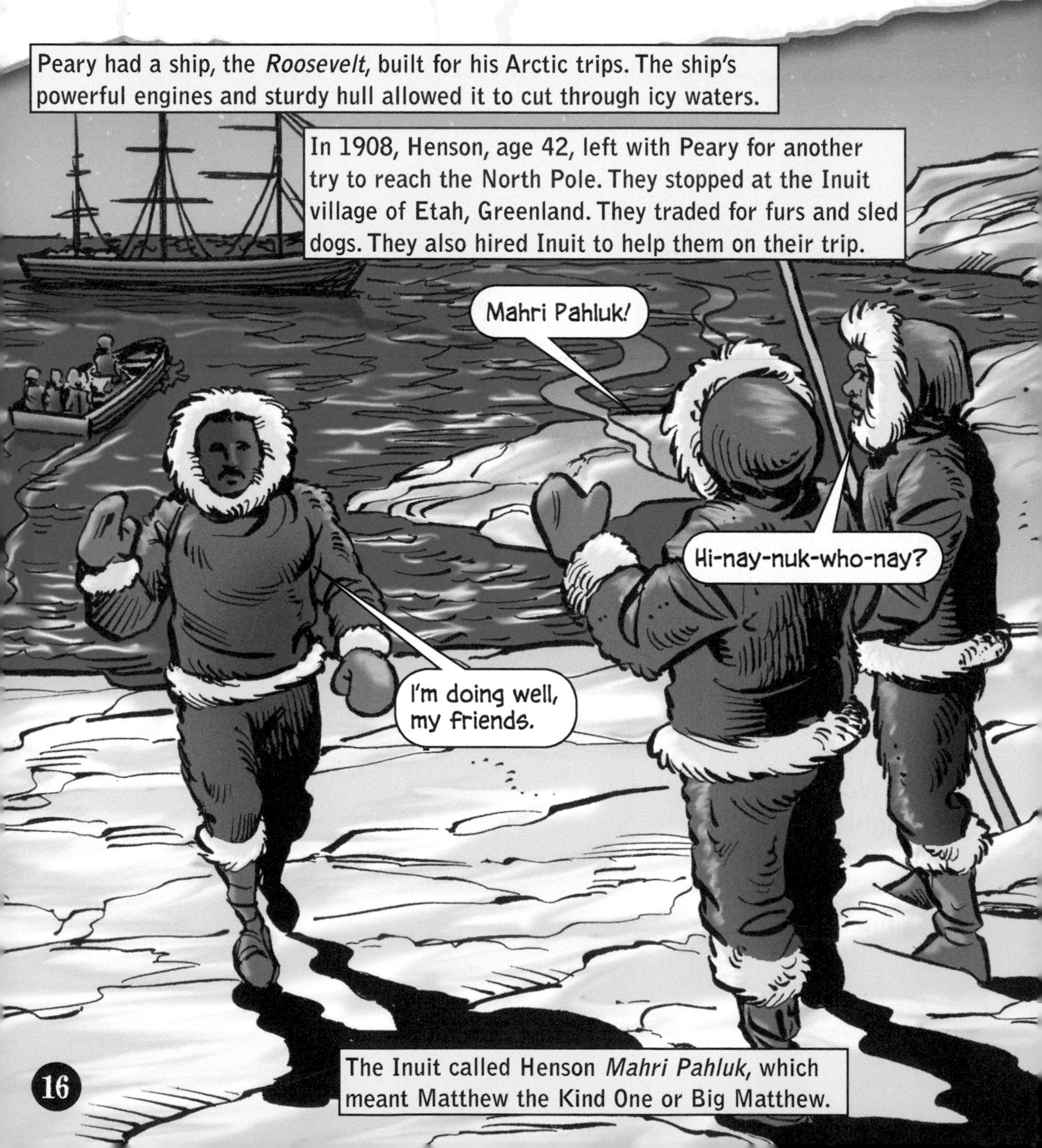
Peary had a ship, the *Roosevelt*, built for his Arctic trips. The ship's powerful engines and sturdy hull allowed it to cut through icy waters.
In 1908, Henson, age 42, left with Peary for another try to reach the North Pole. They stopped at the Inuit village of Etah, Greenland. They traded for furs and sled dogs. They also hired Inuit to help them on their trip.
Mahri Pahluk!
Hi-nay-nuk-who-nay?
I'm doing well, my friends.
The Inuit called Henson *Mahri Pahluk*, which meant Matthew the Kind One or Big Matthew.

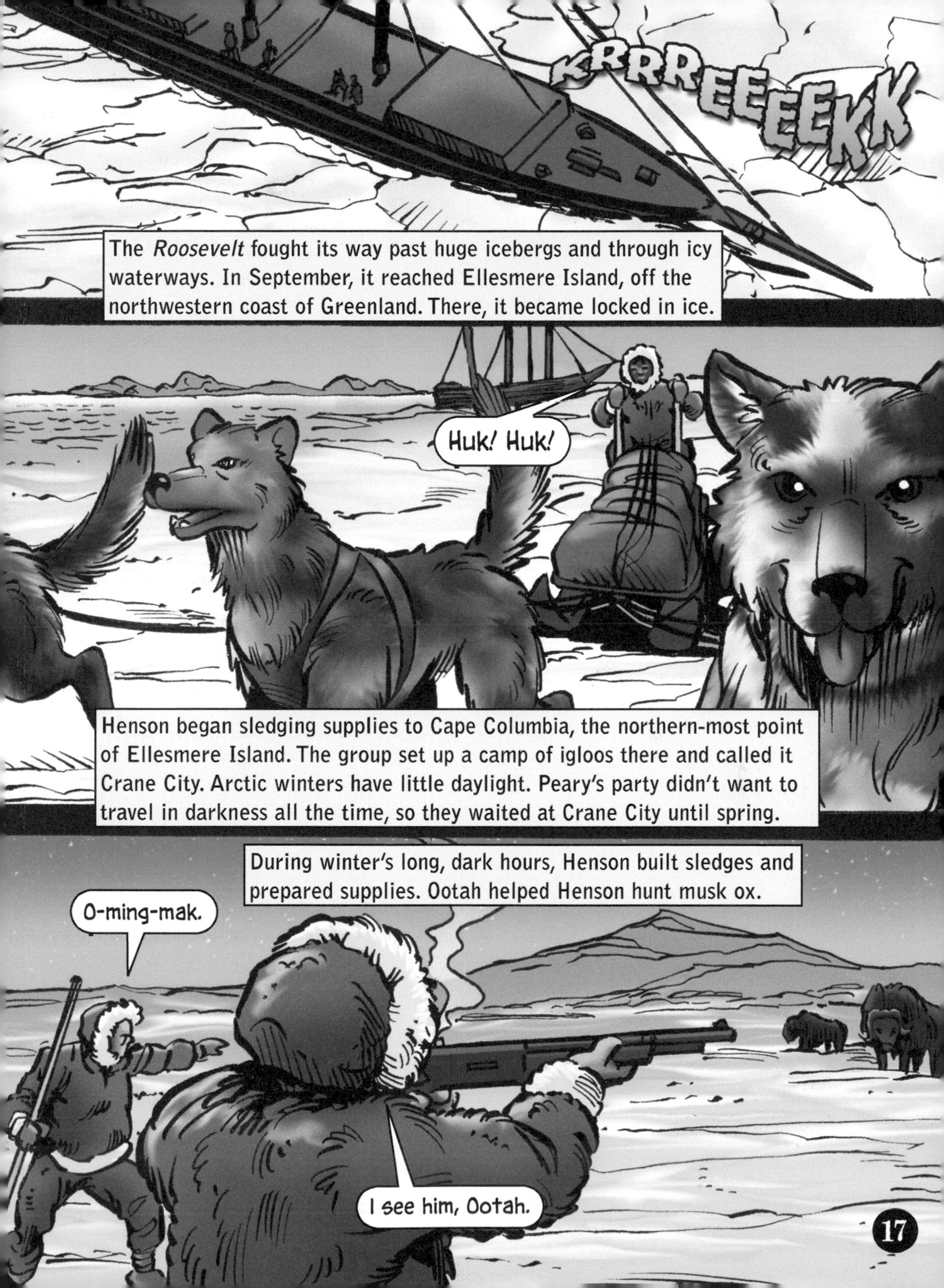
KRRREEEEKK
The *Roosevelt* fought its way past huge icebergs and through icy waterways. In September, it reached Ellesmere Island, off the northwestern coast of Greenland. There, it became locked in ice.
Huk! Huk!
Henson began sledging supplies to Cape Columbia, the northern-most point of Ellesmere Island. The group set up a camp of igloos there and called it Crane City. Arctic winters have little daylight. Peary's party didn't want to travel in darkness all the time, so they waited at Crane City until spring.
During winter's long, dark hours, Henson built sledges and prepared supplies. Ootah helped Henson hunt musk ox.
O-ming-mak.
I see him, Ootah.

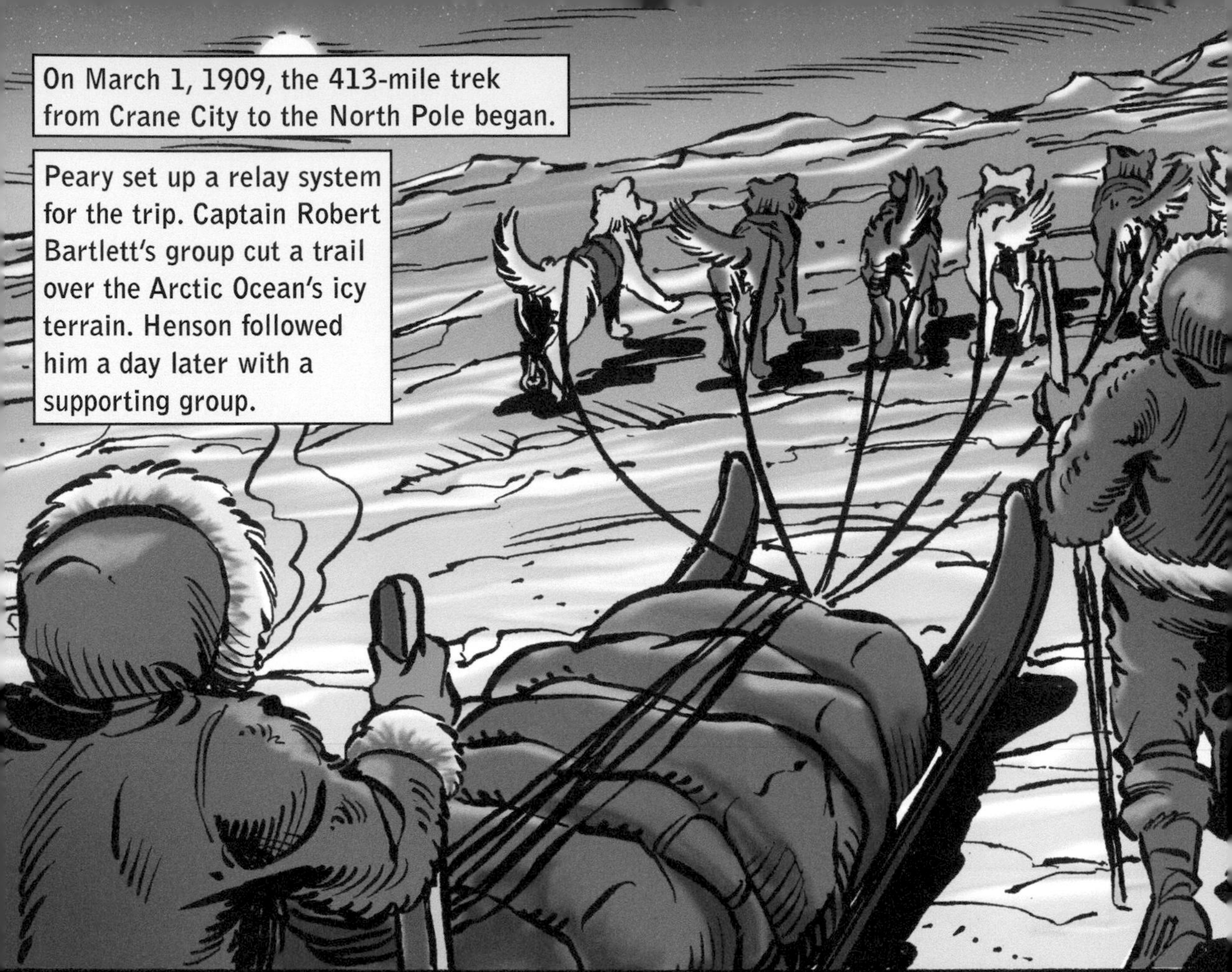
On March 1, 1909, the 413-mile trek from Crane City to the North Pole began.
Peary set up a relay system for the trip. Captain Robert Bartlett's group cut a trail over the Arctic Ocean's icy terrain. Henson followed him a day later with a supporting group.

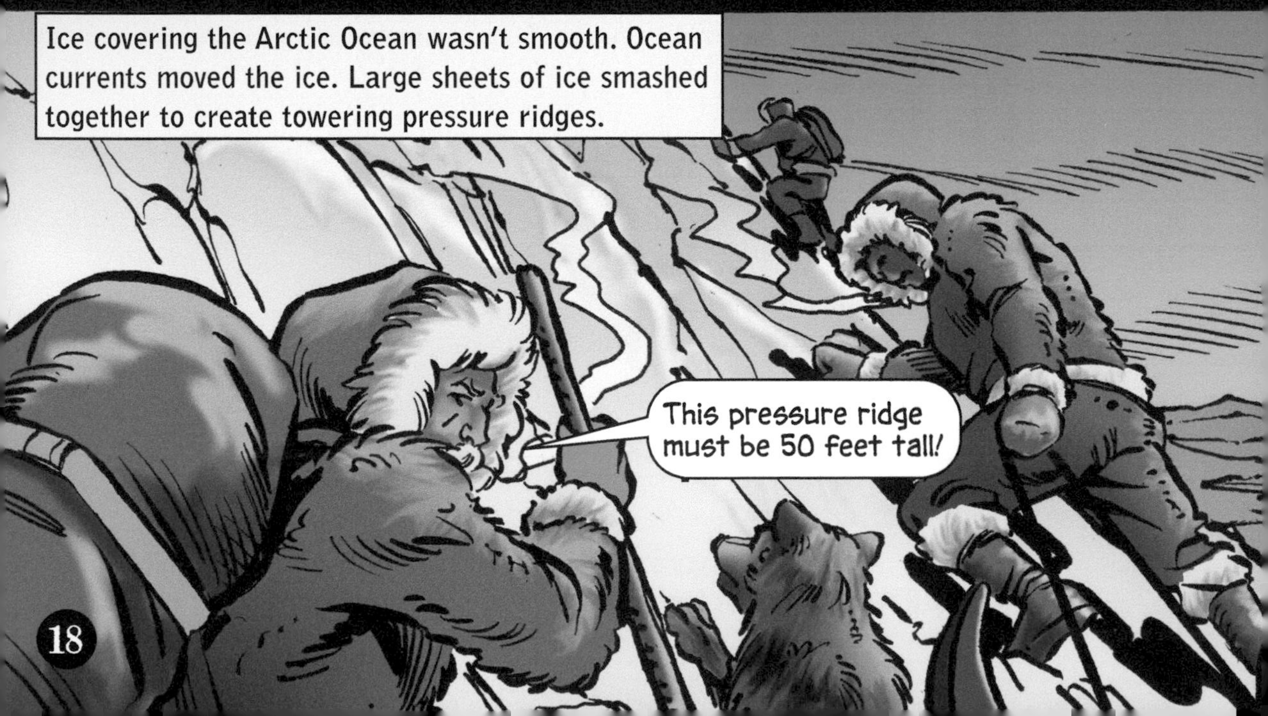
Ice covering the Arctic Ocean wasn't smooth. Ocean currents moved the ice. Large sheets of ice smashed together to create towering pressure ridges.
This pressure ridge must be 50 feet tall!

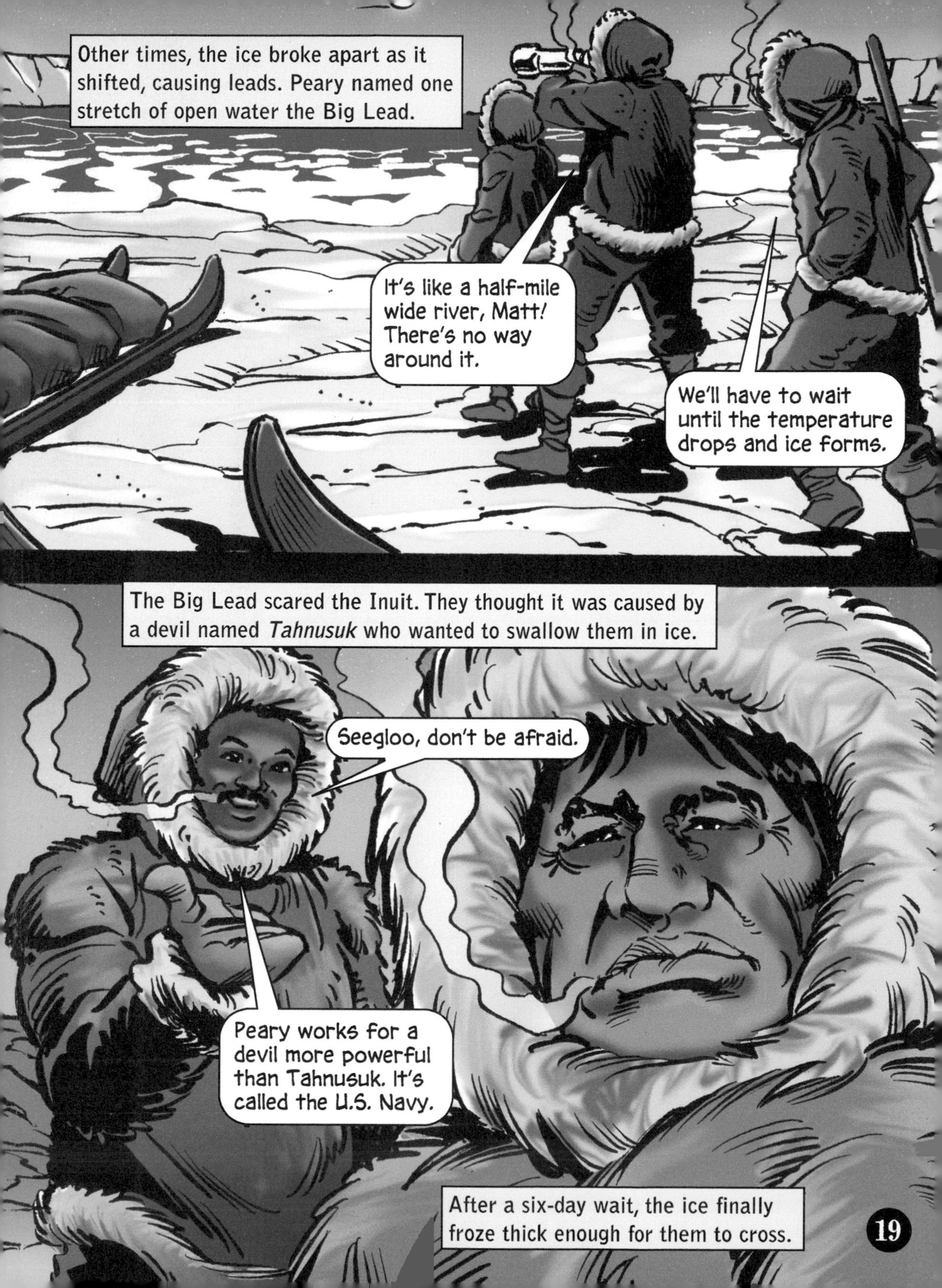
Other times, the ice broke apart as it shifted, causing leads. Peary named one stretch of open water the Big Lead.
It's like a half-mile wide river, Matt! There's no way around it.
We'll have to wait until the temperature drops and ice forms.
The Big Lead scared the Inuit. They thought it was caused by a devil named *Tahnusuk* who wanted to swallow them in ice.
Seegloo, don't be afraid.
Peary works for a devil more powerful than Tahnusuk. It's called the U.S. Navy.
After a six-day wait, the ice finally froze thick enough for them to cross.

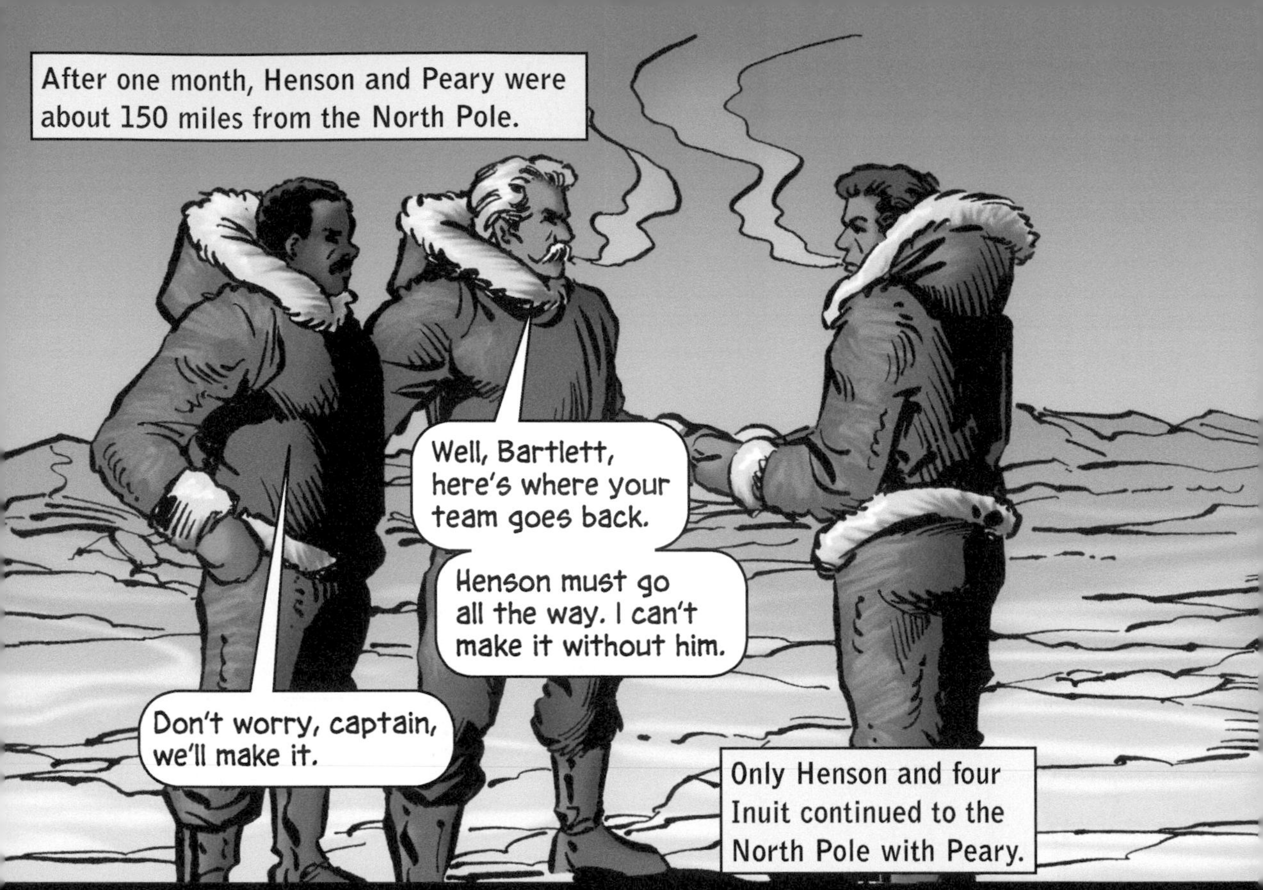
After one month, Henson and Peary were about 150 miles from the North Pole.
Well, Bartlett, here's where your team goes back.
Henson must go all the way. I can't make it without him.
Don't worry, captain, we'll make it.
Only Henson and four Inuit continued to the North Pole with Peary.

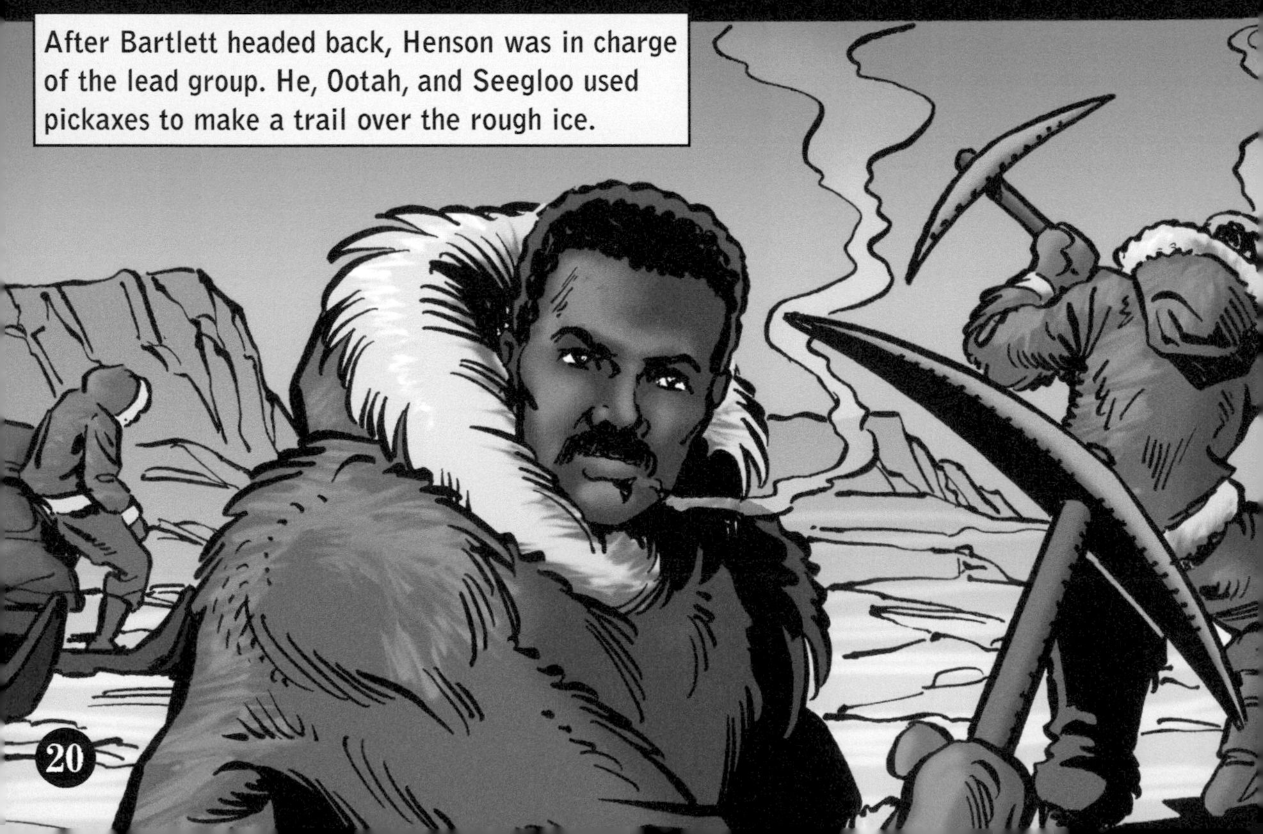
After Bartlett headed back, Henson was in charge of the lead group. He, Ootah, and Seegloo used pickaxes to make a trail over the rough ice.

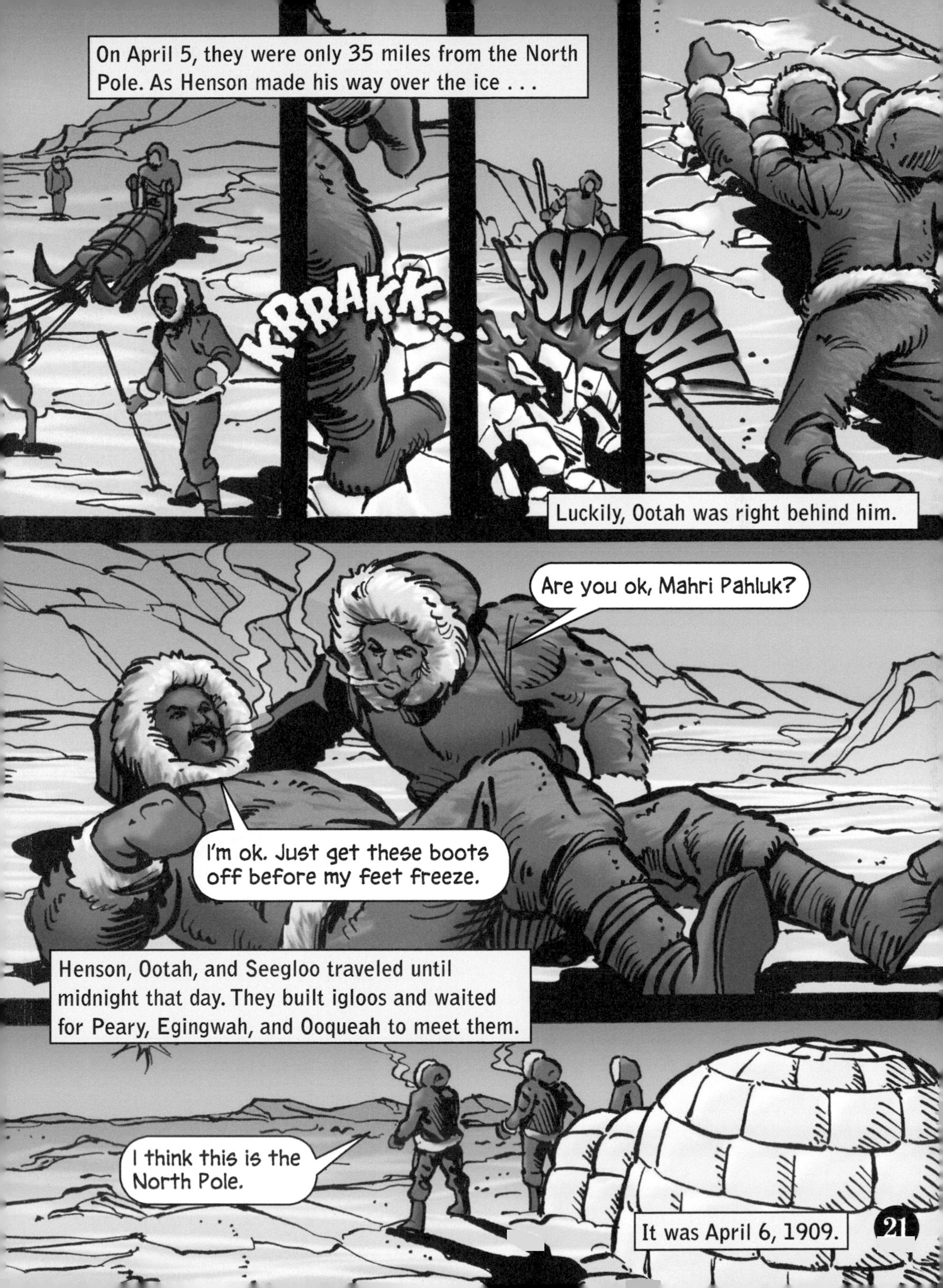
On April 5, they were only 35 miles from the North Pole. As Henson made his way over the ice . . .
KRRAKK...
SPLOOSH!
Luckily, Ootah was right behind him.
Are you ok, Mahri Pahluk?
I'm ok. Just get these boots off before my feet freeze.
Henson, Ootah, and Seegloo traveled until midnight that day. They built igloos and waited for Peary, Egingwah, and Ooqueah to meet them.
I think this is the North Pole.
It was April 6, 1909.

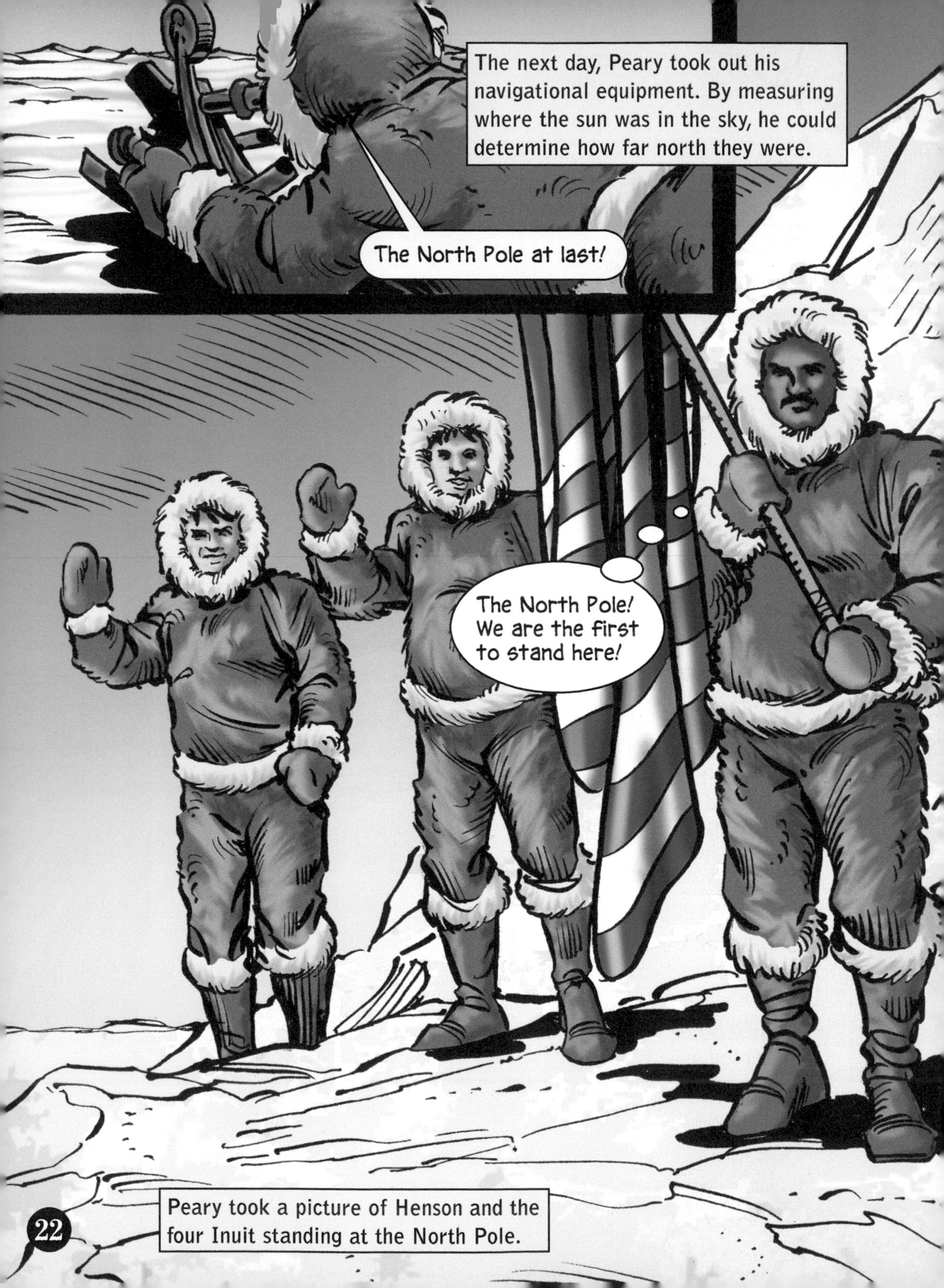
The next day, Peary took out his navigational equipment. By measuring where the sun was in the sky, he could determine how far north they were.
The North Pole at last!
The North Pole! We are the first to stand here!
Peary took a picture of Henson and the four Inuit standing at the North Pole.

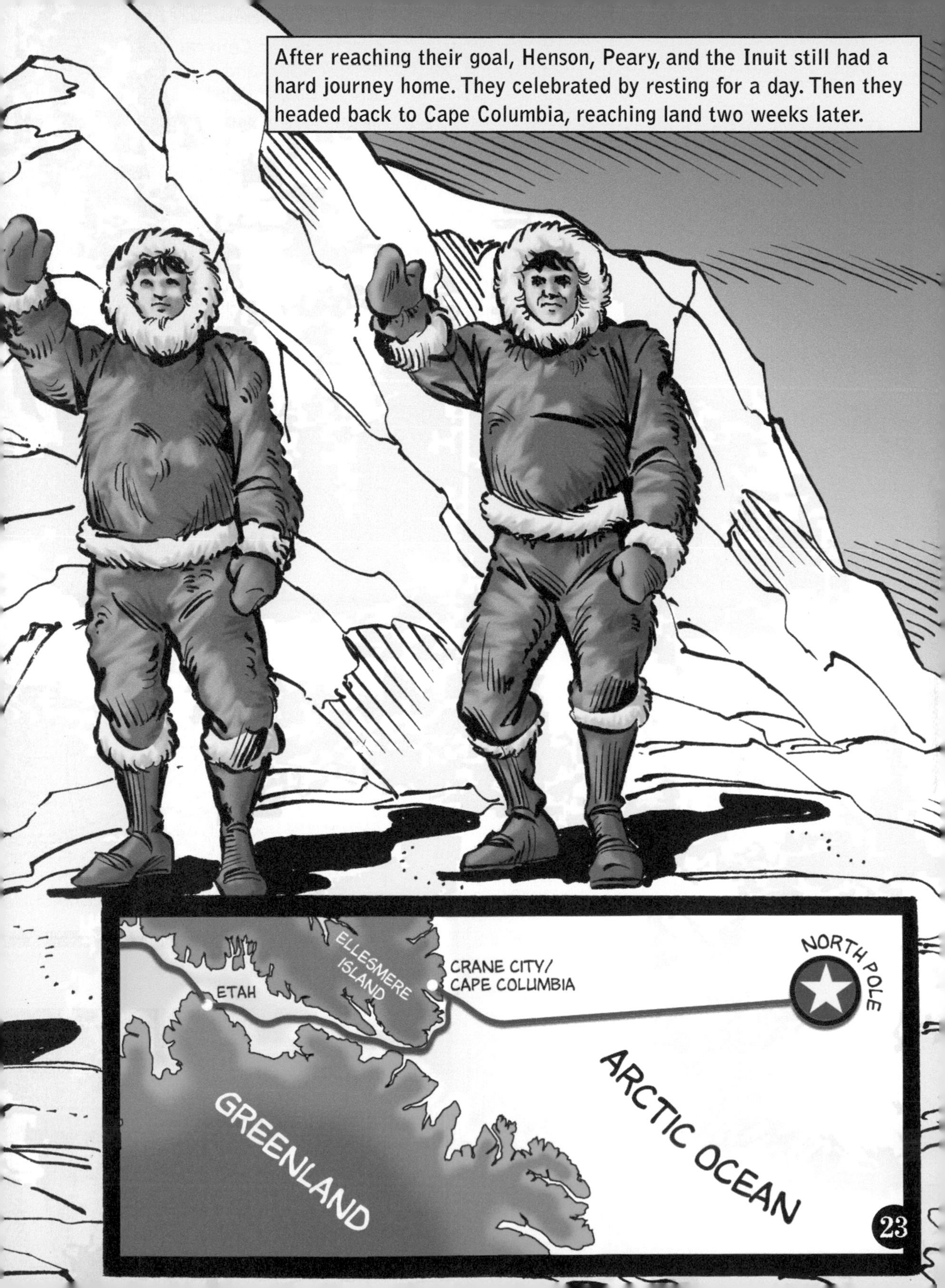
After reaching their goal, Henson, Peary, and the Inuit still had a hard journey home. They celebrated by resting for a day. Then they headed back to Cape Columbia, reaching land two weeks later.
ELLESMERE ISLAND
CRANE CITY/
CAPE COLUMBIA
ETAH
NORTH POLE
ARCTIC OCEAN
GREENLAND

CHAPTER 4 Peary's "Colored Assistant"

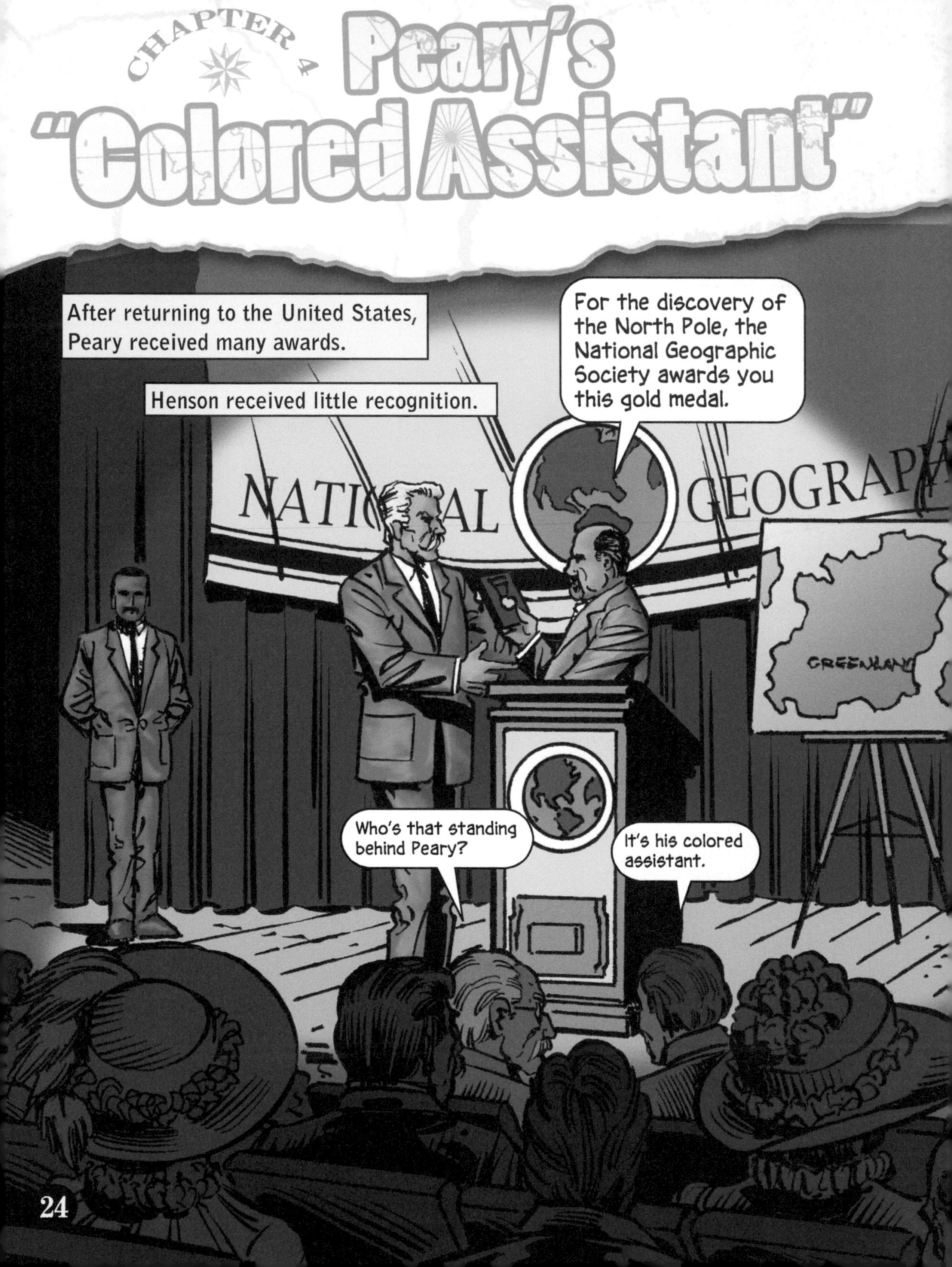
After returning to the United States, Peary received many awards.
Henson received little recognition.
For the discovery of the North Pole, the National Geographic Society awards you this gold medal.
NATIONAL GEOGRAPH
Who's that standing behind Peary?
It's his colored assistant.

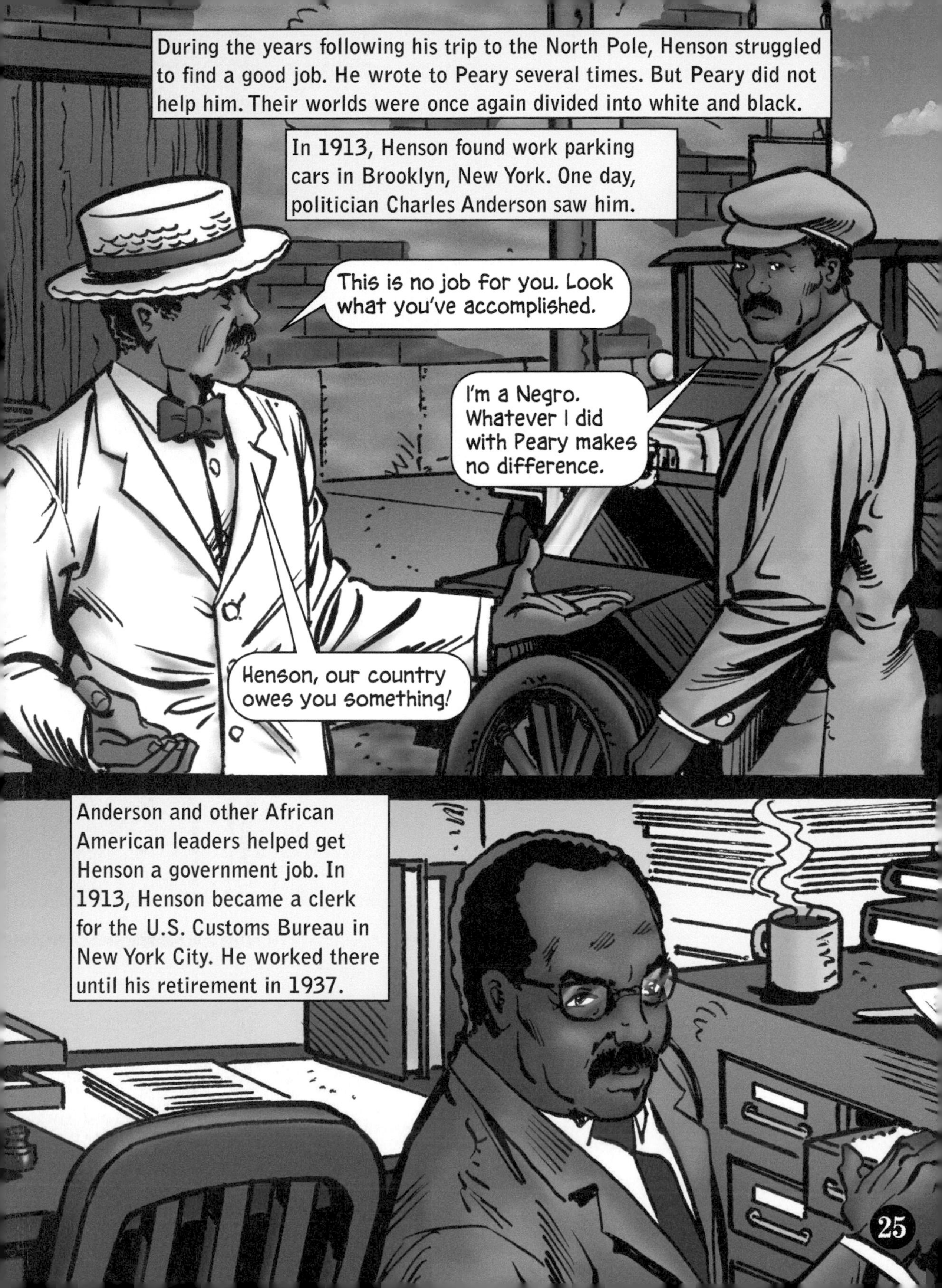
During the years following his trip to the North Pole, Henson struggled to find a good job. He wrote to Peary several times. But Peary did not help him. Their worlds were once again divided into white and black.
In 1913, Henson found work parking cars in Brooklyn, New York. One day, politician Charles Anderson saw him.
This is no job for you. Look what you've accomplished.
I'm a Negro. Whatever I did with Peary makes no difference.
Henson, our country owes you something!
Anderson and other African American leaders helped get Henson a government job. In 1913, Henson became a clerk for the U.S. Customs Bureau in New York City. He worked there until his retirement in 1937.

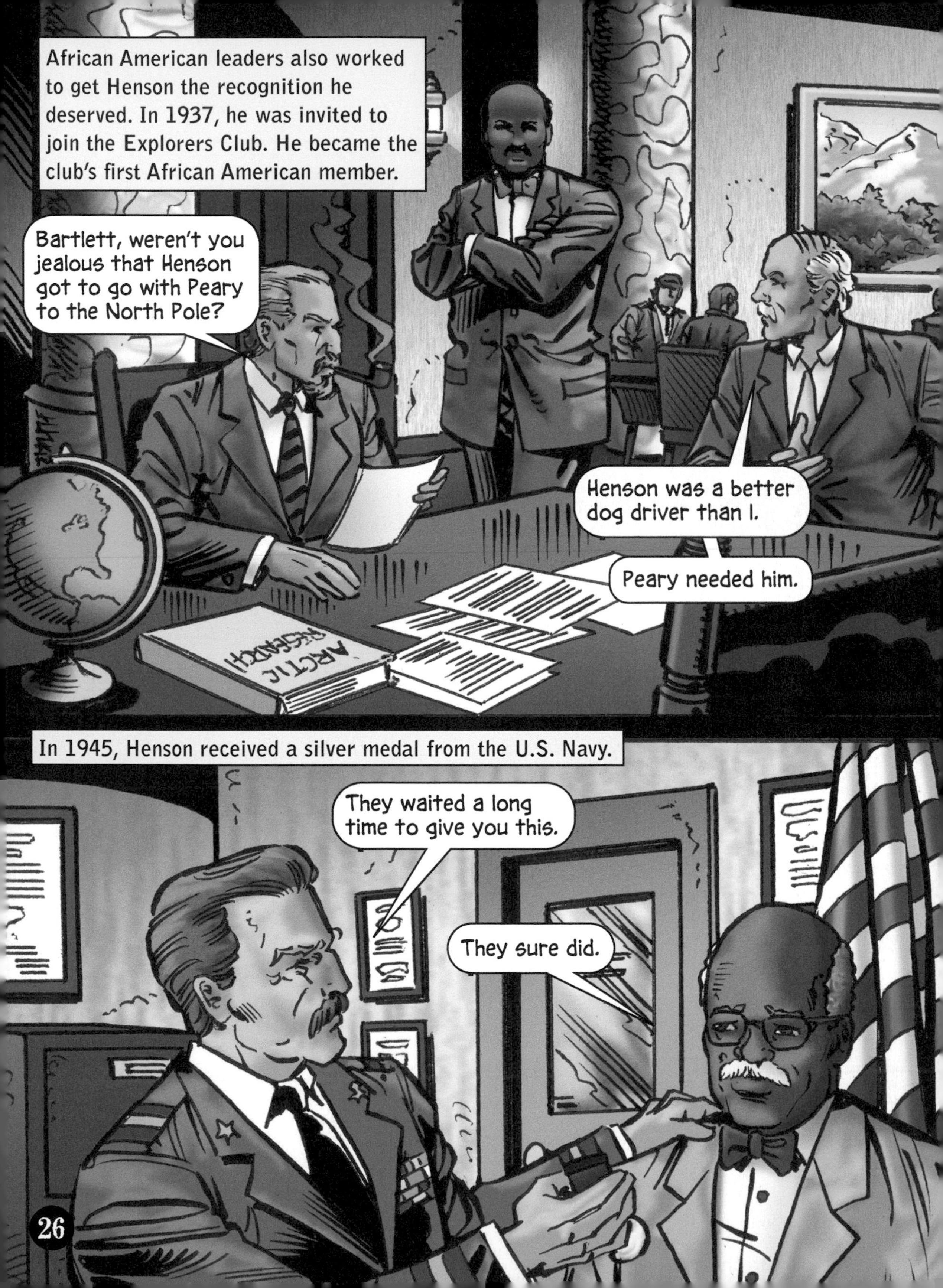
African American leaders also worked to get Henson the recognition he deserved. In 1937, he was invited to join the Explorers Club. He became the club's first African American member.
Bartlett, weren't you jealous that Henson got to go with Peary to the North Pole?
Henson was a better dog driver than I.
Peary needed him.
ARCTIC RESEARCH
In 1945, Henson received a silver medal from the U.S. Navy.
They waited a long time to give you this.
They sure did.

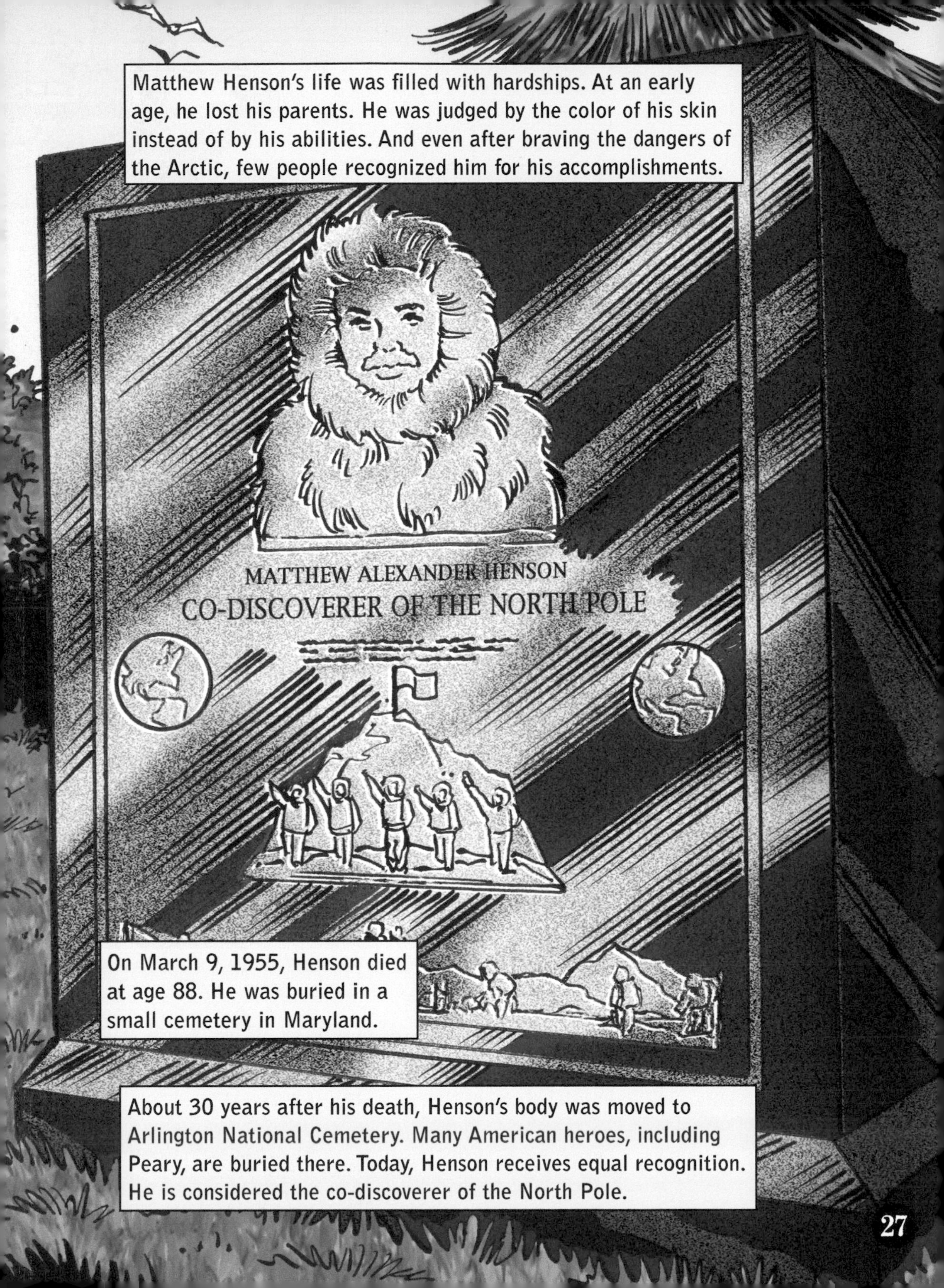
Matthew Henson's life was filled with hardships. At an early age, he lost his parents. He was judged by the color of his skin instead of by his abilities. And even after braving the dangers of the Arctic, few people recognized him for his accomplishments.
MATTHEW ALEXANDER HENSON
CO-DISCOVERER OF THE NORTH POLE
On March 9, 1955, Henson died at age 88. He was buried in a small cemetery in Maryland.
About 30 years after his death, Henson's body was moved to Arlington National Cemetery. Many American heroes, including Peary, are buried there. Today, Henson receives equal recognition. He is considered the co-discoverer of the North Pole.

More about MATTHEW HENSON

✳ Matthew Alexander Henson was born August 8, 1866, near Nanjemoy, Maryland. Henson had two sisters and three brothers.

✳ People aren't sure when Henson's parents died. Good records were not kept for African Americans in the 1800s. But Henson's parents died when he was very young. He was on his own by age 12.

✳ In 1893, Henson adopted an Inuit boy, Kudlooktoo, whose mother had died. He helped take care of Kudlooktoo during his visits to the Arctic. After the 1909 North Pole expedition, Henson lost touch with him.

✳ After the 1893–1895 trip, Henson wasn't sure he wanted to go back to the Arctic. An African American friend, George Gardner, told Henson that he had to go back to prove that African Americans could play an important role in history-making events.

✳ In 1906, Henson had a son, Anaukaq, with an Inuit woman, Akatingwah. Henson never saw them after he left the Arctic in 1909. In 1986, Anaukaq and his sons traveled to the United States to meet some of Henson's relatives.

Henson died March 9, 1955, at age 88.

In 2000, 91 years after the discovery of the North Pole, the National Geographic Society awarded Henson the Hubbard Medal. The organization had given the same award to Peary in 1906.

INUIT GLOSSARY:

- **Hi-nay-nuk-who-nay?**—Hello, how are you?
- **Huk! Huk!**—the command to get sled dogs moving
- **Inuit**—the people
- **Mahri Pahluk**—Matthew the Kind One or Big Matthew
- **O-ming-mak**—musk ox

GLOSSARY

igloo (IG-loo)—the traditional house of the Inuit, made of sod, wood, stone, blocks of ice, or hard snow

Inuit (IN-yoo-it)—native people of the Arctic

lead (LEED)—area of open water on a frozen body of water

porter (POR-tur)—someone who carries luggage for people at a railroad station or hotel

pressure ridge (PRESH-ur RIJ)—tall piles of ice formed by large sheets of ice on the Arctic Ocean that smash together

racism (RAY-sih-zuhm)—the belief that one race is better than another race

sledge (SLEJ)—to drive a dog team; or the sled that is used by a dog team.

torrents (TOR-uhnts)—huge outpourings of something

valet (va-LAY)—a person who attends to the personal needs of another person

INTERNET SITES

FactHound offers a safe, fun way to find Internet sites related to this book. All of the sites on FactHound have been researched by our staff.

Here's how:

1. *Visit www.facthound.com*
2. Type in this special code **0736846344** for age-appropriate sites. Or enter a search word related to this book for a more general search.
3. Click on the **Fetch It** button.

FactHound will fetch the best sites for you!

READ MORE

Armentrout, David, and Patricia Armentrout. *Matthew Henson.* Discover the Life of an American Legend. Vero Beach, Fla.: Rourke, 2004.

Currie, Stephen. *Polar Explorers.* History Makers. San Diego: Lucent, 2002.

Gaines, Ann. *Matthew Henson and the North Pole Expedition.* Journey to Freedom. Chanhassen, Minn: Child's World, 2001.

Litwin, Laura Baskes. *Matthew Henson: Co-discoverer of the North Pole.* African-American Biographies. Berkeley Heights, N.J.: Enslow, 2001.

Weidt, Maryann N. *Matthew Henson.* History Maker Bios. Minneapolis: Lerner, 2003.

BIBLIOGRAPHY

Counter, S. Allen. *North Pole Legacy: Black, White, and Eskimo.* Amherst: University of Massachusetts Press, 1991.

Henson, Matthew. *A Negro Explorer at the North Pole.* Montpelier, Vt.: Invisible Cities Press, 2001.

Peary, Robert E. *The North Pole.* New York: Cooper Square Press, 2001.

Robinson, Bradley. *Dark Companion.* New York: R. M. McBride, 1948.

INDEX